The Crucible

ARTHUR MILLER

Notes and questions by
Maureen Blakesley

Heinemann is an imprint of Pearson Education Limited,
a company incorporated in England and Wales, having
its registered office at Edinburgh Gate, Harlow, Essex, CM20 2JE.
Registered company number: 872828

Earlier version copyright under the title *Those Familiar Spirits*
First published in England in 1956
First published in the *Hereford Plays* series 1967
First published in the *Heinemann Plays* series 1992

47

A catalogue record for this book is available from the British Library on request.

ISBN: 978 0 435 23281 8

Cover photo: Getty
Typeset by TechType, Abingdon, Oxon
Printed in China (SWTC/47)

CONTENTS

PREFACE

In this edition of *The Crucible*, you will find notes, questions and activities to help in studying the play in class, particularly at GCSE level.

The introduction provides background information on the author, the historical basis to the play, the circumstances and impact of its first production and plays by other authors on the same theme.

The activities at the end of the book range from straightforward *Keeping Track* questions which can be tackled at the end of each act to focus close attention on what is happening in the play, through more detailed work on characters and themes in *Explorations*, to more advanced discussion questions under *Criticism*.

There is also a bibliography with details both of Arthur Miller's work and some recent works of criticism and biography. Right at the end of the book is a glossary, arranged by acts, for easy reference.

If you are already using the Hereford edition of *The Crucible*, you will find that the page numbering in the actual playscript is the same, allowing the two editions to be easily used side by side.

INTRODUCTION

Arthur Miller

Arthur Miller was born on 17 October 1915 in New York City and spent the first fourteen years of his life in Harlem. His father, Isidore, had come to America from Austria and had become a prosperous clothing manufacturer. The Stock Market crash of 1929, and the economic depression which followed it, ruined the family business so that when the young Miller graduated from high school in 1932 there was no money to send him to university. He took various jobs to earn money to go to college, working for two years as a shipping clerk in an automobile-parts warehouse in Manhattan.

He applied to the University of Michigan in 1934, at first to study economics and history, but also taking a course in journalism and later on in playwriting. He won several drama awards for plays written at university, the first, *No Villain* based on his own family in New York. After graduating in 1938 he worked in the Brooklyn Navy Yard, at the same time writing for radio. The first really successful stage play was *All My Sons* which opened in 1947 and ran for 328 performances. It was made into a film and produced in other countries too. This was followed by the even more successful *Death of a Salesman* which opened in January 1949 and has been played many times since.

Both these plays deal with the difficulties of an individual in society, and both deal with businessmen coping with the pressures of making a living and at the same time retaining their dignity. Miller believed that tragedy was not confined to the rich and important, but that the story of an ordinary man's failure was just as moving and terrible. Some critics interpreted these plays as attacks on capitalism – even on the American way of life. However, the theatre critic of the *New York Post* summed up the majority view: 'Only the most fatuous observer could think of *Death of a*

Salesman as a propaganda play and yet it manages to go deeply enough into contemporary values to be valid and frightening social criticism.'

Arthur Miller's next play *The Crucible* was first produced in 1953 in the middle of the McCarthy political 'witch-hunt' in America although the story had appealed to the playwright for many years. This meant that it was seen as a political parable.

McCarthyism

Since 1938 an organisation called the House Un-American Activities Committee had been in existence in America. This had the power to investigate any movement or person who apparently threatened the safety of the state. Under the chairmanship of Senator Joseph McCarthy, this committee became almost paranoid in its searching out of communist sympathisers amongst the American people in the late 1940s and early 1950s.

The Second World War had ended in 1945 and during the next five or ten years two enormous power blocs faced each other, the United States of America and the USSR. America was fighting in Korea in an attempt to stem the tide of communism in Asia and as each side grew more threatening and belligerent, there were real fears in America that the philosophy of communism was spreading there and would eventually undermine and destroy capitalism and the American way of life.

Almost any criticism of the government or its instructions became, in the eyes of McCarthy, an admission of adherence to communism. Witnesses were brought before the committee to answer charges that they were communist sympathisers and, more importantly, to name those whom they had seen at meetings or discussions held perhaps ten, even twenty, years earlier. Liberal writers, film directors and actors all appeared before the committee and as a result many of them found it impossible to work in the American theatre or film industry again.

In 1956, when the power of the committee was waning, Miller was summoned to appear before it. A pile of petitions with his signature was produced and he was asked to confess to signing his name. 'In truth, I had supported these various causes to express my fear of a looming victory of fascism and my alienation from the waste of potential in America while knowing nothing about life under any socialist regime.'

The activities of the Committee began to be linked in Miller's mind with witchcraft trials which had taken place in the American town of Salem two centuries before. For example, the Committee often had in its possession lists of people at various meetings, and yet it still wanted the witnesses to name names. Miller saw these public confessions as parallels with the naming of names at Salem in 1692:

> 'The political question, therefore, of whether witches and communists could be equated was no longer to the point. What was manifestly parallel was the guilt, two centuries apart, of holding illicit, suppressed feelings of alienation and hostility toward standard, daylight society as defined by its most orthodox proponents.'

Witchcraft in Salem

In his autobiography *Timebends*, Arthur Miller tells us that he had known about the witchcraft phenomenon at Salem since his college days, 'but it had remained in mind as one of those inexplicable mystifications of the long-dead past when people commonly believed that the spirit could leave the body, palpably and visibly'. Then, a copy of Marion Starkey's book *The Devil in Massachusetts* fell into his hands and the seeds were sown for his play *The Crucible*.

As a result of some amateur dabbling in the supernatural by a group of adolescent girls in Salem, Massachusetts in 1692, the jails were eventually filled with men and women accused of witchcraft and twenty people were hanged. To understand this phenomenon, we have to remember that the inhabitants of Salem believed in witches and the Devil and also believed that the Bible had instructed them that witches must be hanged.

The girls were joined by a West Indian slave, Tituba, with her spells and beliefs. Probably more serious was the intervention of Mrs Putnam, seven of whose children died on the nights of their births, and who sent her surviving daughter to Tituba's gatherings to call back their spirits to name their murderers.

Eventually Betty Parris, the daughter of the minister, started to behave like a child possessed, lying in a trance and sometimes crawling around like an animal with her cousin, Abigail Williams. Their behaviour was probably what we would now call 'psychosomatic' but in seventeenth-century Salem, the only explanation was that the children were indeed possessed by the Devil.

In court a hysteria seized the girls as they discovered their power in naming innocent people as accomplices of the Devil. There was, of course, no refuting their accusations because, as Danforth explains in the play, the only witnesses to the witchcraft were the children themselves. Anyone sceptical either about witchcraft or of the truth of the accusations was liable to the same fate and it is not surprising to learn that so many confessed to the sin of trafficking with the Devil when the only alternative was to be hanged.

The seeds of this terrifying event had grown in the fertile ground of a society under great pressure both to defend its Christian way of life in a new continent and to defend its very life against attacks by Indians in the land behind them. The only safeguard against evil of all kinds was felt to lie in a strict code of laws imposing conformity on all its inhabitants. There was no room in Salem for individuality.

In naming people, the girls were probably projecting their own guilt on to the innocent. One such innocent was Elizabeth Proctor, who was accused by her former maid, Abigail Williams. Miller was particularly impressed by the testimony that Abigail Williams when confronted by Elizabeth Proctor stretched out her hand and:

"'immediately, Abigail cried out her fingers, her fingers, her fingers burned . . ." [The girl realised her power over Elizabeth] and experienced the joyous terror of the killer about to strike, and not only at the individual victim, . . . but at the whole society that was watching and applauding her valiant courage in ridding it of its pestilential sins.'

Elizabeth's husband, John Proctor, becomes the central character in the play. Called on to denounce his own wife, his friends and neighbours and finally himself, he goes through an ordeal by conscience, eventually accepting his own death rather than make a false confession.

Historical accuracy

The play is prefixed by Miller's own note on the historical accuracy of the play explaining that dramatic licence has allowed him to condense the number of characters involved and to raise Abigail's age from twelve so that the plot might go ahead. He emphasises that his aim is to show 'the essential nature of one of the strangest and most awful chapters in human history'. The story is well documented in the records of the court proceedings still held in Salem today.

Historical parallels

When Miller was summoned before the House Un-American Activities Committee, he was placed in almost exactly the same position as John Proctor had been in *The Crucible*: he was asked to give names of people he had seen at a meeting of communist writers ten years before. Just as Proctor had done, he refused to answer that question 'as I would not violate what on the spur of the moment I said was my sense of myself'.

In an interview with Christopher Bigsby thirty-five years later, Miller played down the parallel by insisting that 'I was just trying to stay out of jail'. The fact is that since he had not pleaded the Fifth Amendment which protected conscience, he could actually have been sent to jail. In the end he was fined for contempt of Congress.

Miller himself did not want to push the parallel too far and was relieved when in 1965 he overheard a member of the audience not quite recalling the play's links with an American Senator. 'Overhearing, I felt as though I had returned from the dead, and it felt good.'

At the end of the play text Miller roots the story in history once more with the post-script 'Echoes Down the Corridor'. But even more concrete was the contemporary parallel of McCarthy's 'witch-hunt' against communist sympathisers which in 1953 was in full swing.

The title

A crucible is a container in which metals are heated to extract the pure element from dross or impurities. In the play, John Proctor is tested in a life-threatening ordeal and his death at the end rather than betrayal of his conscience shows us that he too has come through the fire to be purified.

Other plays on the same theme

The Crucible's obvious precursor was George Bernard Shaw's *St Joan* which also featured a protagonist at odds with society, a lengthy trial scene and a despatch to martyrdom off-stage.

In 1950 Miller himself had written an adaptation of Ibsen's *An Enemy of the People* dealing with 'the individual who insists that he is right while the vast majority is absolutely wrong'. The play had been a commercial failure and some critics, without knowing the original, had assumed the play to be an attack on America. Miller said nothing, 'hopelessly aware that nothing would burn off the fog of suspicion that I had used Ibsen as a front for the Reds'.

Since 1953 the most obviously similar theme has been in Robert Bolt's *A Man For All Seasons* in which Sir Thomas More is eventually brought to trial for apparently obstructing Henry VIII's marriage to Ann Boleyn. More's trust in the sanctity of the law and his belief that in keeping silent lies his safety are destroyed by Henry's henchman, Thomas Cromwell, who rides rough-shod over both. This play too has a trial, considerable legal debate and the execution of the 'hero'.

Like *St Joan* and *The Crucible*, *A Man For All Seasons* is based on a real historical happening. In all three cases the audience comes to value and applaud the stand made by the individual against the apparent vindictiveness of the law.

The Play in Performance

Many people regard *Death of a Salesman* as Miller's greatest play but *The Crucible* is more widely performed. It is, in fact, performed all over the world because its theme is universal – an individual's stand for what he believes to be morally right against the threats of an immoral society. Miller commented:

'The Crucible became by far my most frequently produced play, both abroad and at home. Its meaning is somewhat different in different places and moments. I can almost tell what the political situation in a country is when the play is suddenly a hit there – it is either a warning of tyranny on the way or a reminder of tyranny just past.'

Unlike Shakespeare's political plays which are also played all over the world and also often underline a relevant contemporary struggle or victory, *The Crucible* has always been played exactly in its historical context with Puritan clothes and sets similar to those of the original production, and is never 'updated'. It is very distinctly 'of its time' and yet still maintains its relevance because of its theme.

Writing in 1990 in a collection of essays as a tribute to Miller on his seventy-fifth birthday, John Arden wrote, 'Miller, in short, with *The Crucible*, moved the theatrical re-creation of history forward in one great stride of English language.' At the time of its first performance in 1953 the play was hailed by many as a great success and yet another triumph for the playwright although he himself was disappointed by the critical reaction:

'No critic seemed to sense what I was after [which was] the conflict between a man's raw deeds and his conception of himself; the question of whether conscience is in fact an organic part of the human being, and what happens when it is handed over not merely to the state or the mores of the time but to one's friend or wife.'

Miller was not only disappointed by the critical reviews but also at 'the hostility in the New York audience'. He eventually redirected it and 'played it all in black, with white lights that never moved from beginning to end'. But it was not a commercial success in spite of the redirection.

Within two years, however, a new production with exactly the same text ran in New York for nearly two years. The play had not changed but the climate of opinion had. 'The metaphor of the immortal underlying forces that can always rise again was now an admissible thing for the press to consider.'

The Language of the Play

Arthur Miller's starting-point for the story of the witches of Salem was the actual court records of the time in which the evidence of the witnesses and all the court proceedings are minutely transcribed. The speech patterns are distinctive. In his auto-biography *Timebends* Miller discusses the language of these court records. 'I wanted to study the actual words of the interrogations, a gnarled way of speaking . . . and I came to love its feel like hard, burnished wood. Without planning to, I even elaborated a few of the grammatical forms myself, the double negatives especially.'

The vocabulary and syntax given to the characters in the play are highly dependent on the language of the King James ('Authorised') version of the Bible. When Elizabeth tells John of Mary Warren's visit to the town, she describes the effect of Abigail with an image from the Old Testament: 'Abigail brings the other girls into court, and where she walks the crowd will part like the sea for Israel.'

Many of the images are heightened and important as befits the subject-matter of the play. Danforth states that he would 'hang ten thousand that dared to rise against the law, and an ocean of salt tears could not melt the resolution of the statutes'. John Proctor describes his farm as 'a continent', Elizabeth's behaviour as 'an everlasting funeral' and her justice which 'would freeze beer'. The language is powerful, evocative and memorable. At important moments such as the last few minutes of the play, the language is monosyllabic like the beat of a drum. 'What profit him to bleed? Shall the dust praise him? Shall the worms declare his truth? Go to him, take his shame away!'

Many of the verbs are used archaically, apparently distancing the characters from their twentieth-century audience. The very first words we hear are 'My Betty be hearty soon?' from Tituba and soon we hear 'It were sport, uncle!' and 'There be no blush about my name'. Everyone speaks with the same dialect: Danforth asks 'did you not tell me Mary Warren were sick in bed'? There is an archaic use too in addressing men as 'Mister' and women as 'Goody' – short for Good Wife. All of this contributes to the feeling of a different society – distanced not only by time but by the way it communicated.

When the play is acted there is the problem of finding an accent for the actors although the distinctive speech patterns written by Miller almost enforce an accent. He recounts that Laurence Olivier, searching for a way in which to speak the words, 'decided on a Northumberland dialect, which indeed is spoken through clenched jaws'.

Even though the play is set in America, the date is 1692 and the distinctive American accent, so influenced by the Irish immigrants of the nineteenth century, had not developed. It was only 70 years before that the ancestors of the inhabitants of Salem had arrived in America, and their speech and accent were still very like the British ones of the time.

Maureen Blakesley

A Note on the Historical Accuracy of the Play

This play is not history in the sense in which the word is used by the academic historian. Dramatic purposes have sometimes required many characters to be fused into one; the number of girls invclved in the 'crying out' has been reduced; Abigail's age has been raised; while there were several judges of almost equal authority, I have symbolized them all in Hathorne and Danforth. However, I believe that the reader will discover here the essential nature of one of the strangest and most awful chapters in human history. The fate of each character is exactly that of his historical model, and there is no one in the drama who did not play a similar – and in some cases exactly the same – role in history.

As for the characters of the persons, little is known about most of them excepting what may be surmised from a few letters, the trial record, certain broadsides written at the time, and references to their conduct in sources of varying reliability. They may therefore be taken as creations of my own, drawn to the best of my ability in conformity with their known behaviour, except as indicated in the commentary I have written for this text.

ARTHUR MILLER

List of Characters

BETTY PARRIS
REVEREND SAMUEL PARRIS
TITUBA
ABIGAIL WILLIAMS
SUSANNA WALCOTT
GOODWIFE ANN PUTNAM
THOMAS PUTNAM
MERCY LEWIS
MARY WARREN
JOHN PROCTOR
GOODWIFE REBECCA NURSE
GILES COREY
REVEREND JOHN HALE
GOODWIFE ELIZABETH PROCTOR
FRANCIS NURSE
EZEKIEL CHEEVER
MARSHAL HERRICK
DEPUTIES
JUDGE HATHORNE
DEPUTY-GOVERNOR DANFORTH

Cast of the 1965 National Theatre Production

The Crucible was first presented at the Martin Beck Theatre, New York, in January 1953. Direction was by Jed Harris. In England it was first performed at the Theatre Royal, Bristol, directed by Warren Jenkins, in November 1954. George Devine directed the first London production at the Royal Court Theatre in April 1956. The play was included in the repertory of the National Theatre in January 1965, produced by Sir Laurence Olivier, with the following cast:

BETTY PARRIS	*Janina Faye*
REVEREND SAMUEL PARRIS	*Kenneth Mackintosh*
TITUBA	*Pearl Prescod*
ABIGAIL WILLIAMS	*Louise Purnell*
SUSANNA WALCOTT	*Janie Booth*
GOODWIFE ANN PUTNAM	*Barbara Hicks*
THOMAS PUTNAM	*Trevor Martin*
MERCY LEWIS	*Sheila Reed*
MARY WARREN	*Jeanne Hepple*
JOHN PROCTOR	*Colin Blakely*
GOODWIFE REBECCA NURSE	*Wynne Clark*
GILES COREY	*Frank Finlay*
REVEREND JOHN HALE	*Robert Lang*
GOODWIFE ELIZABETH PROCTOR	*Joyce Redman*
FRANCIS NURSE	*Keith Marsh*
EZEKIEL CHEEVER	*Michael Turner*
MARSHAL HERRICK	*James Mellor*
DEPUTIES	*Mike Gambon*
	Robert Russell
JUDGE HATHORNE	*Peter Cellier*
DEPUTY-GOVERNOR DANFORTH	*Anthony Nicholls*

Scenery and Costumes by MICHAEL ANNALS

ACT ONE

*A small upper bedroom in the home of Reverend Samuel
Parris, Salem, Massachusetts, in the spring of the year 1692.
There is a narrow window at the left. Through its leaded
panes the morning sunlight streams. A candle still burns
near the bed, which is at the right. A chest, a chair, and a
small table are the other furnishings. At the back a door
opens on the landing of the stairway to the ground floor. The
room gives off an air of clean spareness. The roof rafters are
exposed, and the wood colours are raw and unmellowed.
As the curtain rises,* REVEREND PARRIS *is discovered kneeling
beside the bed, evidently in prayer. His daughter* BETTY PARRIS,
aged ten, is lying on the bed, inert.

At the time of these events Parris was in his middle
forties. In history he cut a villainous path, and there is very
little good to be said for him. He believed he was being
persecuted wherever he went, despite his best efforts to win
people and God to his side. In meetings, he felt insulted if
someone rose to shut the door without first asking his
permission. He was a widower with no interest in children,
or talent with them. He regarded them as young adults, and
until this strange crisis he, like the rest of Salem, never
conceived that the children were anything but thankful for
being permitted to walk straight, eyes slightly lowered, arms
at the sides, and mouths shut until bidden to speak.

His house stood in the 'town' – but we today would hardly
call it a village. The meeting house was nearby, and from this
point outward – toward the bay or inland – there were a few
small-windowed, dark houses snuggling against the raw Massachusetts winter. Salem had been established hardly forty years

before. To the European world the whole province was a barbaric frontier inhabited by a sect of fanatics who, nevertheless, were shipping out products of slowly increasing quantity and value.

No one can really know what their lives were like. They had no novelists – and would not have permitted anyone to read a novel if one were handy. Their creed forbade anything resembling a theatre or 'vain enjoyment'. They did not celebrate Christmas, and a holiday from work meant only that they must concentrate even more upon prayer.

Which is not to say that nothing broke into this strict and sombre way of life. When a new farmhouse was built, friends assembled to 'raise the roof', and there would be special foods cooked and probably some potent cider passed around. There was a good supply of ne'er-do-wells in Salem, who dallied at the shovelboard in Bridget Bishop's tavern. Probably more than the creed, hard work kept the morals of the place from spoiling, for the people were forced to fight the land like heroes for every grain of corn, and no man had very much time for fooling around.

That there were some jokers, however, is indicated by the practice of appointing a two-man patrol whose duty was to 'walk forth in the time of God's worship to take notice of such as either lye about the meeting house, without attending to the word and ordinances, or that lye at home or in the fields without giving good account there of, and to take the names of such persons, and to present them to the magistrates, whereby they may be accordingly proceeded against'. This predilection for minding other people's business was time-honoured among the people of Salem, and it undoubtedly created many of the suspicions which were to feed the coming madness. It was also, in my opinion, one of the things that a John Proctor would rebel against, for the time of the armed camp had almost passed, and since the country was reasonably – although not wholly – safe, the old disciplines were beginning to rankle. But, as in all such matters, the issue was not clear-cut, for danger was still a possibility, and in unity still lay the best promise of safety.

The edge of the wilderness was close by. The American continent stretched endlessly west, and it was full of mystery for them. It stood, dark and threatening, over their shoulders night and day, for out of it Indian tribes marauded from time to time, and Reverend Parris had parishioners who had lost relatives to these heathen.

The parochial snobbery of these people was partly responsible for their failure to convert the Indians. Probably they also preferred to take land from the heathens rather than from fellow Christians. At any rate, very few Indians were converted, and the Salem folk believed that the virgin forest was the Devil's last preserve, his home base and the citadel of his final stand. To the best of their knowledge the American forest was the last place on earth that was not paying homage to God.

For these reasons, among others, they carried about an air of innate resistance, even of persecution. Their fathers had, of course, been persecuted in England. So now they and their church found it necessary to deny any other sect its freedom, lest their New Jerusalem be defiled and corrupted by wrong ways and deceitful ideas.

They believed, in short, that they held in their steady hands the candle that would light the world. We have inherited this belief, and it has helped and hurt us. It helped them with the discipline it gave them. They were a dedicated folk, by and large, and they had to be to survive the life they had chosen or been born into in this country.

The proof of their belief's value to them may be taken from the opposite character of the first Jamestown settlement, farther south, in Virginia. The Englishmen who landed there were motivated mainly by a hunt for profit. They had thought to pick off the wealth of the new country and then return rich to England. They were a band of individualists, and a much more ingratiating group than the Massachusetts men. But Virginia destroyed them. Massachusetts tried to kill off the Puritans, but they combined; they set up a communal society which, in the beginning, was little more than an armed camp with an autocratic and very devoted leadership. It was, however, an autocracy by consent, for they were united from top to bottom by a commonly held ideology whose perpetuation was the reason and justification for all their sufferings. So their self-denial, their purposefulness, their suspicion of all vain pursuits, their hardhanded justice, were altogether perfect instruments for the conquest of this space so antagonistic to man.

But the people of Salem in 1692 were not quite the dedicated folk that arrived on the *Mayflower*. A vast differentiation had taken place, and in their own time a revolution had unseated the royal government and substituted a junta which was at this moment in power. The times, to their eyes, must have been out of joint, and to the common folk must have seemed as insoluble and complicated as do ours today. It is not hard to see how easily many could have been led to believe that the time of confusion had been brought upon them by deep and darkling forces. No hint of such speculation appears on the court record, but social disorder in any age breeds such mystical suspicions, and when, as in Salem, wonders are brought forth from below the social surface, it is too much to expect people to hold back very long from laying on the victims with all the force of their frustrations.

The Salem tragedy, which is about to begin in these pages, developed from a paradox. It is a paradox in whose grip we still live, and there is no prospect yet that we will discover its resolution. Simply, it was this: for good purposes, even high purposes, the people of Salem developed a theocracy, a combine of state and religious power whose function was to keep the community together, and to prevent any kind of disunity that might open it to destruction by material or ideological enemies. It was forged for a necessary purpose and accomplished that purpose. But all organization is and must be grounded on the idea of exclusion and prohibition, just as two objects cannot occupy the same space. Evidently the time came in New England when the repressions of order were heavier than seemed warranted by the dangers against which the order was organized. The witch-hunt was a perverse manifestation of the panic which set in among all classes when the balance began to turn toward greater individual freedom.

When one rises above the individual villainy displayed, one can only pity them all, just as we shall be pitied someday. It is still impossible for man to organize his social life without repressions, and the balance has yet to be struck between order and freedom.

The witch-hunt was not, however, a mere repression. It was also, and as importantly, a long overdue opportunity for everyone so inclined to express publicly his guilt and sins, under the cover of accusations against the victims. It suddenly became possible – and patriotic and holy – for a man to say that Martha Corey had come into his bedroom at night, and that, while his wife was sleeping at his side, Martha laid herself down on his chest and 'nearly suffocated him'. Of course it was her spirit only, but his satisfaction at confessing himself was no lighter than if it had been Martha herself. One could not ordinarily speak such things in public.

Long-held hatreds of neighbours could now be openly expressed, and vengeance taken, despite the Bible's charitable injunctions. Land-lust which had been expressed before by constant bickering over boundaries and deeds, could now be elevated to the arena of morality; one could cry witch against one's neighbour and feel perfectly justified in the bargain. Old scores could be settled on a plane of heavenly combat between Lucifer and the Lord; suspicions and the envy of the miserable toward the happy could and did burst out in the general revenge.

REVEREND PARRIS is *praying now, and, though we cannot hear his words, a sense of his confusion hangs about him. He mumbles,*

*then seems about to weep; then he prays again; but his
daughter does not stir on the bed.*

*The door opens, and his Negro slave enters. Tituba is in her
forties. Parris brought her with him from Barbados, where he
spent some years as a merchant before entering the ministry.
She enters as one does who can no longer bear to be barred
from the sight of her beloved, but she is also very frightened
because her slave sense has warned her that, as always,
trouble in this house eventually lands on her back.*

TITUBA (*already taking a step backward*): My Betty be hearty soon?

PARRIS Out of here!

TITUBA (*backing to the door*): My Betty not goin' die . . .

PARRIS (*scrambling to his feet in a fury*): Out of my sight! (*She is
gone.*) Out of my – (*He is overcome with sobs. He clamps
his teeth against them and closes the door and leans against
it, exhausted.*) Oh, my God! God help me! (*Quaking with
fear, mumbling to himself through his sobs, he goes to the bed
and gently takes Betty's hand.*) Betty. Child. Dear child.
Will you wake, will you open up your eyes! Betty, little
one . . .

He is bending to kneel again when his niece, ABIGAIL
WILLIAMS, *seventeen, enters – a strikingly beautiful girl, an
orphan, with an endless capacity for dissembling. Now she is
all worry and apprehension and propriety.*

ABIGAIL Uncle? (*He looks to her.*) Susanna Walcott's here from
Doctor Griggs.

PARRIS Oh? Let her come, let her come.

ABIGAIL (*leaning out the door to call to Susanna, who is down the
hall a few steps*): Come in, Susanna.

SUSANNA WALCOTT, *a little younger than Abigail, a
nervous, hurried girl, enters.*

PARRIS (*eagerly*): What does the doctor say, child?

SUSANNA (*craning around Parris to get a look at Betty*): He bid me
come and tell you, reverend sir, that he cannot discover
no medicine for it in his books.

PARRIS Then he must search on.

SUSANNA   Aye, sir, he have been searchin' his books since he left you, sir. But he bid me tell you, that you might look to unnatural things for the cause of it.

PARRIS   (*his eyes going wide*): No – no. There be no unnatural cause here. Tell him I have sent for Reverend Hale of Beverly, and Mr Hale will surely confirm that. Let him look to medicine and put out all thought of unnatural causes here. There be none.

SUSANNA   Aye, sir. He bid me tell you. (*She turns to go.*)

ABIGAIL   Speak nothin' of it in the village, Susanna.

PARRIS   Go directly home and speak nothing of unnatural causes.

SUSANNA   Aye, sir. I pray for her. (*She goes out.*)

ABIGAIL   Uncle, the rumour of witchcraft is all about; I think you'd best go down and deny it yourself. The parlour's packed with people, sir. I'll sit with her.

PARRIS   (*pressed, turns on her*): And what shall I say to them? That my daughter and my niece I discovered dancing like heathen in the forest?

ABIGAIL   Uncle, we did dance; let you tell them I confessed it – and I'll be whipped if I must be. But they're speakin' of witchcraft. Betty's not witched.

PARRIS   Abigail, I cannot go before the congregation when I know you have not opened with me. What did you do with her in the forest?

ABIGAIL   We did dance, uncle, and when you leaped out of the bush so suddenly, Betty was frightened and then she fainted. And there's the whole of it.

PARRIS   Child. Sit you down.

ABIGAIL   (*quavering, as she sits*): I would never hurt Betty. I love her dearly.

PARRIS   Now look you, child, your punishment will come in its time. But if you trafficked with spirits in the forest I must know it now, for surely my enemies will, and they will ruin me with it.

ABIGAIL   But we never conjured spirits.

PARRIS   Then why can she not move herself since midnight?

This child is desperate! (ABIGAIL *lowers her eyes.*) It must
come out – my enemies will bring it out. Let me know what
you done there. Abigail, do you understand that I have
many enemies?

ABIGAIL   I have heard of it, uncle.

PARRIS   There is a faction that is sworn to drive me from my pulpit.
Do you understand that?

ABIGAIL   I think so, sir.

PARRIS   Now then, in the midst of such disruption, my own
household is discovered to be the very centre of some
obscene practice. Abominations are done in the forest –

ABIGAIL   It were sport, uncle!

PARRIS   (*pointing at Betty*): You call this sport? (*She lowers her eyes.
He pleads.*) Abigail, if you know something that may help
the doctor, for God's sake tell it to me. (*She is silent.*) I saw
Tituba waving her arms over the fire when I came on you.
Why was she doing that? And I heard a screeching and
gibberish coming from her mouth. She were swaying like a
dumb beast over that fire!

ABIGAIL   She always sings her Barbados songs, and we dance.

PARRIS   I cannot blink what I saw, Abigail, for my enemies will not
blink it. I saw a dress lying on the grass.

ABIGAIL   (*innocently*): A dress?

PARRIS   – (*it is very hard to say*): Aye, a dress. And I thought I saw –
someone naked running through the trees!

ABIGAIL   (*in terror*): No one was naked! You mistake yourself, uncle!

PARRIS   (*with anger*): I saw it! (*He moves from her. Then, resolved.*)
Now tell me true, Abigail. And I pray you feel the weight of
truth upon you, for now my ministry's at stake, my ministry
and perhaps your cousin's life. Whatever abomination you
have done, give me all of it now, for I dare not be taken
unaware when I go before them down there.

ABIGAIL   There is nothin' more. I swear it, uncle.

PARRIS   (*studies her, then nods, half convinced*): Abigail, I have fought
here three long years to bend these stiff-necked people to me,

and now, just now when some good respect is rising for me in the parish, you compromise my very character. I have given you a home, child, I have put clothes upon your back – now give me upright answer. Your name in the town – it is entirely white, is it not?

ABIGAIL (*with an edge of resentment*): Why, I am sure it is, sir. There be no blush about my name.

PARRIS (*to the point*): Abigail, is there any other cause than you have told me, for your being discharged from Goody Proctor's service? I have heard it said, and I tell you as I heard it, that she comes so rarely to church this year for she will not sit so close to something soiled. What signified that remark?

ABIGAIL She hates me, uncle, she must, for I would not be her slave. It's a bitter woman, a lying, cold, snivelling, woman, and I will not work for such a woman!

PARRIS She may be. And yet it has troubled me that you are now seven month out of their house, and in all this time no other family has ever called for your service.

ABIGAIL They want slaves, not such as I. Let them send to Barbados for that. I will not black my face for any of them! (*With ill-concealed resentment at him.*) Do you begrudge my bed, uncle?

PARRIS No –no.

ABIGAIL (*in a temper*): My name is good in the village! I will not have it said my name is soiled! Goody Proctor is a gossiping liar!

Enter MRS ANN PUTNAM. *She is a twisted soul of forty-five, a death-ridden woman, haunted by dreams.*

PARRIS (*as soon as the door begins to open*): No – no, I cannot have anyone. (*He sees her, and a certain deference springs into him, although his worry remains.*) Why, Goody Putnam, come in.

MRS PUT'M (*full of breath, shiny-eyed*): It is a marvel. It is surely a stroke of hell upon you.

PARRIS No, Goody Putnam, it is–

MRS PUT'M (*glancing at Betty*): How high did she fly, how high?

PARRIS No, no, she never flew–

MRS PUT'M (*very pleased with it*): Why, it's sure she did. Mr

Collins saw her goin' over Ingersoll's barn, and come down light as a bird, he says!

PARRIS Now, look you, Goody Putnam, she never – (*Enter* THOMAS PUTNAM, *a well-to-do, hard-handed landowner, near fifty.*) Oh, good morning, Mr Putnam.

PUTNAM It is a providence the thing is out now! It is a providence. (*He goes directly to the bed.*)

PARRIS What's out, sir, what's–?

MRS PUTNAM *goes to the bed.*

PUTNAM (*looking down at Betty*): Why, her eyes is closed! Look you, Ann.

MRS PUT'M Why, that's strange. (*To Parris.*) Ours is open.

PARRIS (*shocked*): Your Ruth is sick?

MRS PUT'M (*with vicious certainty*): I'd not call it sick; the Devil's touch is heavier than sick. It's death, y'know, it's death drivin' into them, forked and hoofed.

PARRIS Oh, pray not! Why, how does Ruth ail?

MRS PUT'M She ails as she must – she never waked this morning, but her eyes open and she walks, and hears naught, sees naught, and cannot eat. Her soul is taken, surely.

PARRIS *is struck.*

PUTNAM (*as though for further details*): They say you've sent for Reverend Hale of Beverly?

PARRIS (*with dwindling conviction now*): A precaution only. He has much experience in all demonic arts, and I –

MRS PUT'M He has indeed; and found a witch in Beverly last year, and let you remember that.

PARRIS Now, Goody Ann, they only thought that were a witch, and I am certain there be no element of witchcraft here.

PUTNAM No witchcraft! Now look you, Mr Parris –

PARRIS Thomas, Thomas, I pray you, leap not to witchcraft. I know that you – you least of all, Thomas, would ever wish so disastrous a charge laid upon me. We cannot leap to witchcraft. They will howl me out of Salem for such corruption in my house.

A word about Thomas Putnam. He was a man with many grievances, at least one of which appears justified. Some time before, his wife's brother-in-law, James Bayley, had been turned down as minister of Salem. Bayley had all the qualifications, and a two-thirds vote into the bargain, but a faction stopped his acceptance, for reasons that are not clear.

Thomas Putnam was the eldest son of the richest man in the village. He had fought the Indians at Narragansett, and was deeply interested in parish affairs. He undoubtedly felt it poor payment that the village should so blatantly disregard his candidate for one of its more important offices, especially since he regarded himself as the intellectual superior of most of the people around him.

His vindictive nature was demonstrated long before the witchcraft began. Another former Salem minister, George Burroughs, had had to borrow money to pay for his wife's funeral, and, since the parish was remiss in his salary, he was soon bankrupt. Thomas and his brother John had Burroughs jailed for debts the man did not owe. The incident is important only in that Burroughs succeeded in becoming minister where Bayley, Thomas Putnam's brother-in-law, had been rejected; the motif of resentment is clear here. Thomas Putnam felt that his own name and the honour of his family had been smirched by the village, and he meant to right matters however he could.

Another reason to believe him a deeply embittered man was his attempt to break his father's will, which left a disproportionate amount to a stepbrother. As with every other public cause in which he tried to force his way, he failed in this.

So it is not surprising to find that so many accusations against people are in the handwriting of Thomas Putnam, or that his name is so often found as a witness corroborating the supernatural testimony, or that his daughter led the crying-out at the most opportune junctures of the trials, especially when– But we'll speak of that when we come to it.

PUTNAM (*at the moment he is intent upon getting Parris, for whom he has only contempt, to move toward the abyss*): Mr Parris, I have taken your part in all contention here, and I would continue; but I cannot if you hold back in this. There are hurtful, vengeful spirits layin' hands on these children.

PARRIS But, Thomas, you cannot–

PUTNAM Ann! Tell Mr Parris what you have done.

MRS PUT'M Reverend Parris, I have laid seven babies unbaptized in the earth. Believe me, sir, you never saw more hearty babies born. And yet, each would wither in my arms the very night of their birth. I have spoke nothin', but my heart has clamoured intimations. And now, this year, my Ruth, my only–I see her turning strange. A secret child she has become this year, and shrivels like a sucking mouth were pullin' on her life too. And so I thought to send her to your Tituba–

PARRIS To Tituba! What may Tituba–?

MRS PUT'M Tituba knows how to speak to the dead, Mr Parris.

PARRIS Goody Ann, it is a formidable sin to conjure up the dead!

MRS PUT'M I take it on my soul, but who else may surely tell us what person murdered my babies?

PARRIS (*horrified*): Woman!

MRS PUT'M They were murdered, Mr Parris! And mark this proof! Mark it! Last night my Ruth were ever so close to their little spirits; I know it, sir. For how else is she struck dumb now except some power of darkness would stop her mouth? It is a marvellous sign, Mr Parris!

PUTNAM Don't you understand it, sir? There is a murdering witch among us, bound to keep herself in the dark. (PARRIS *turns to Betty, a frantic terror rising in him.*) Let your enemies make of it what they will, you cannot blink it more.

PARRIS (*to Abigail*): Then you were conjuring spirits last night.

ABIGAIL (*whispering*): Not I, sir–Tituba and Ruth.

PARRIS (*turns now, with new fear, and goes to Betty, looks down at her, and then gazing off*): Oh, Abigail, what proper payment for my charity! Now I am undone.

PUTNAM   You are not undone! Let you take hold there. Wait for no
              one to charge you – declare it yourself. You have
              discovered witchcraft–

PARRIS   In my house? In my house, Thomas? They will topple me
              with this! They will make of it a–

              Enter MERCY LEWIS, *the Putnam's servant, a fat, sly, merciless
              girl of eighteen.*

MERCY   Your pardons. I only thought to see how Betty is.

PUTNAM   Why aren't you home? Who's with Ruth?

MERCY   Her grandma come. She's improved a little, I think–she give
              a powerful sneeze before.

MRS PUT'M Ah, there's a sign of life?

MERCY   I'd fear no more, Goody Putnam. It were a grand sneeze;
              another like it will shake her wits together, I'm sure. (*She
              goes to the bed to look.*)

PARRIS   Will you leave me now, Thomas? I would pray a while
              alone.

ABIGAIL   Uncle, you've prayed since midnight. Why do you not go
              down and–

PARRIS   No–no. (*To Putnam*): I have no answer for that crowd. I'll
              wait till Mr Hale arrives. (*To get Mrs Putnam to leave.*) If you
              will, Goody Ann . . .

PUTNAM   Now look you, sir. Let you strike out against the Devil, and
              the village will bless you for it! Come down, speak to
              them–pray with them. They're thirsting for your word,
              Mister! Surely you'll pray with them.

PARRIS   (*swayed*): I'll lead them in a psalm, but let you say nothing
              of witchcraft yet. I will not discuss it. The cause is yet
              unknown. I have had enough contention since I came; I
              want no more.

MRS PUT'M Mercy, you go home to Ruth, d'y'hear?

MERCY   Aye, mum.

              MRS PUTNAM *goes out.*

PARRIS   (*to Abigail*): If she starts for the window, cry for me at once.

ABIGAIL   I will, uncle.

PARRIS   (*to Putnam*): There is a terrible power in her arms today.
              He goes out with Putnam.

ABIGAIL (*with hushed trepidation*): How is Ruth sick?

MERCY   It's weirdish, I know not–she seems to walk like a dead one
              since last night.

ABIGAIL (*turns at once and goes to Betty, and now, with fear in her
              voice*): Betty? (BETTY *doesn't move. She shakes her.*) Now stop
              this! Betty! Sit up now!

              BETTY *doesn't stir.* MERCY *comes over.*

MERCY   Have you tried beatin' her? I gave Ruth a good one and it
              waked her for a minute. Here, let me have her.

ABIGAIL (*holding Mercy back*): No, he'll be comin' up. Listen, now; if
              they be questioning us, tell them we danced–I told him as
              much already.

MERCY   Aye. And what more?

ABIGAIL He knows Tituba conjured Ruth's sisters to come out of the
              grave.

MERCY   And what more?

ABIGAIL He saw you naked.

MERCY   (*clapping her hands together with a frightened laugh*): Oh,
              Jesus!

              Enter MARY WARREN, *breathless. She is seventeen, a subservient,
              naive, lonely girl.*

MARY   What'll we do? The village is out! I just come from the farm:
              the whole country's talkin' witchcraft! They'll be callin' us
              witches, Abby!

MERCY   (*pointing and looking at Mary Warren*): She means to tell, I
              know it.

MARY   Abby, we've got to tell. Witchery's a hangin' error, a hangin'
              like they done in Boston two year ago! We must tell the
              truth, Abby! You'll only be whipped for dancin', and the
              other things!

ABIGAIL Oh, *we'll* be whipped!

MARY   I never done none of it, Abby. I only looked!

MERCY   (*moving menacingly toward Mary*): Oh, you're a great one for lookin', aren't you, Mary Warren? What a grand peeping courage you have!

BETTY, *on the bed, whimpers.* ABIGAIL *turns to her at once.*

ABIGAIL Betty? (*She goes to Betty.*) Now, Betty, dear, wake up now. It's Abigail. (*She sits Betty up and furiously shakes her.*) I'll beat you, Betty! (BETTY *whimpers.*) My, you seem improving. I talked to your papa and told him everything. So there's nothing to—

BETTY (*darts off the bed, frightened of Abigail, and flattens herself against the wall*): I want my mama!

ABIGAIL (*with alarm, as she cautiously approaches Betty*): What ails you Betty? Your mama's dead and buried.

BETTY I'll fly to Mama. Let me fly! (*She raises her arms as though to fly, and streaks for the window, gets one leg out.*)

ABIGAIL (*pulling her away from the window*): I told him everything; he knows now, he knows everything we—

BETTY You drank blood, Abby! You didn't tell him that!

ABIGAIL Betty, you never say that again! You will never—

BETTY You did, you did! You drank a charm to kill John Proctor's wife! You drank a charm to kill Goody Proctor!

ABIGAIL (*smashes her across the face*): Shut it! Now shut it!

BETTY (*collapsing on the bed*): Mama, Mama! (*She dissolves into sobs.*)

ABIGAIL Now look you. All of you. We danced. And Tituba conjured Ruth Putnam's dead sisters. And that is all. And mark this. Let either of you breathe a word, or the edge of a word, about the other things, and I will come to you in the black of some terrible night and I will bring a pointy reckoning that will shudder you. And you know I can do it: I saw Indians smash my dear parents' heads on the pillow next to mine, and I have seen some reddish work done at night, and I can make you wish you had never seen the sun go down! (*She goes to Betty and roughly sits her up.*) Now, you—sit up and stop this!

But BETTY *collapses in her hands and lies inert on the bed.*

MARY (*with hysterical fright*): What's got her? (ABIGAIL *stares in fright at Betty.*) Abby, she's going to die! It's a sin to conjure, and we–

ABIGAIL (*starting for Mary*): I say shut it, Mary Warren!

Enter JOHN PROCTOR. *On seeing him,* MARY WARREN *leaps in fright.*

Proctor was a farmer in his middle thirties. He need not have been a partisan of any faction in the town, but there is evidence to suggest that he had a sharp and biting way with hypocrites. He was a kind of man–powerful of body, even-tempered, and not easily led–who cannot refuse support to partisans without drawing their deepest resentment. In Proctor's presence a fool felt his foolishness instantly – and a Proctor is always marked for calumny therefore.

But as we shall see, the steady manner he displays does not spring from an untroubled soul. He is a sinner, a sinner not only against the moral fashion of the time, but against his own vision of decent conduct. These people had no ritual for the washing away of sins. It is another trait we inherited from them, and it has helped to discipline us as well as to breed hypocrisy among us. Proctor, respected and even feared in Salem, has come to regard himself as a kind of fraud. But no hint of this has yet appeared on the surface, and as he enters from the crowded parlour below it is a man in his prime we see, with a quiet confidence and an unexpressed, hidden force. Mary Warren, his servant, can barely speak for embarrassment and fear.

MARY Oh! I'm just going home, Mr Proctor.

PROCTOR Be you foolish, Mary Warren? Be you deaf? I forbid you leave the house, did I not? Why shall I pay you? I am looking for you more often than my cows!

MARY I only come to see the great doings in the world.

PROCTOR I'll show you a great doin' on your arse one of these days. Now get you home; my wife is waitin' with your work!

(*Trying to retain a shred of dignity, she goes slowly out.*)

MERCY   (*both afraid of him and strangely titillated*): I'd best be off. I
         have my Ruth to watch. Good morning, Mr Proctor.

         MERCY *sidles out. Since Proctor's entrance,* ABIGAIL *has stood
         as though on tiptoe, absorbing his presence, wide-eyed. He
         glances at her, then goes to Betty on the bed.*

ABIGAIL Gah! I'd almost forgot how strong you are, John
         Proctor!

PROCTOR (*looking at Abigail now, the faintest suggestion of a
         knowing smile on his face*): What's this mischief here?

ABIGAIL (*with a nervous laugh*): Oh, she's only gone silly some-
         how.

PROCTOR The road past my house is a pilgrimage to Salem all
         morning. The town's mumbling witchcraft.

ABIGAIL Oh, posh! (*Winningly she comes a little closer, with a
         confidential, wicked air.*) We were dancin' in the woods
         last night, and my uncle leaped in on us. She took fright, is
         all.

PROCTOR (*his smile widening*): Ah, you're wicked yet, aren't y'! (*A
         trill of expectant laughter escapes her, and she dares come
         closer, feverishly looking into his eyes.*) You'll be clapped in
         the stocks before you're twenty.

         He takes a step to go, and she springs into his path.

ABIGAIL Give me a word, John. A soft word. (*Her concentrated
         desire destroys his smile.*)

PROCTOR No, no, Abby. That's done with.

ABIGAIL (*tauntingly*): You come five mile to see a silly girl fly? I
         know you better.

PROCTOR (*setting her firmly out of his path*): I come to see what
         mischief your uncle's brewin' now. (*With final emphasis.*)
         Put it out of mind, Abby.

ABIGAIL (*grasping his hand before he can release her*): John–I am
         waitin' for you every night.

PROCTOR Abby, I never give you hope to wait for me.

ABIGAIL (*now beginning to anger–she can't believe it*): I have
         something better than hope, I think!

PROCTOR Abby, you'll put it out of mind. I'll not be comin' for you more.

ABIGAIL You're surely sportin' with me.

PROCTOR You know me better.

ABIGAIL I know how you clutched my back behind your house and sweated like a stallion whenever I come near! Or did I dream that? It's she put me out, you cannot pretend it were you. I saw your face when she put me out, and you loved me then and you do now!

PROCTOR Abby, that's a wild thing to say–

ABIGAIL A wild thing may say wild things. But not so wild, I think. I have seen you since she put me out; I have seen you nights.

PROCTOR I have hardly stepped off my farm this seven-month.

ABIGAIL I have a sense for heat, John, and yours has drawn me to my window, and I have seen you looking up, burning in your loneliness. Do you tell me you've never looked up at my window?

PROCTOR I may have looked up.

ABIGAIL (*now softening*): And must you. You are no wintry man. I know you, John. I *know* you. (*She is weeping.*) I cannot sleep for dreamin'; I cannot dream but I wake and walk about the house as though I'd find you comin' through some door. (*She clutches him desperately.*)

PROCTOR (*gently pressing her from him, with great sympathy but firmly*): Child–

ABIGAIL (*with a flash of anger*): How do you call me child!

PROCTOR Abby, I may think of you softly from time to time. But I will cut off my hand before I'll ever reach for you again. Wipe it out of mind. We never touched, Abby.

ABIGAIL Aye, but we did.

PROCTOR Aye, but we did not.

ABIGAIL (*with a bitter anger*): Oh, I marvel how such a strong man may let such a sickly wife be–

PROCTOR   (*angered–at himself as well*): You'll speak nothin' of
           Elizabeth!

ABIGAIL   She is blackening my name in the village! She is telling lies
           about me! She is a cold, snivelling woman, and you bend to
           her! Let her turn you like a–

PROCTOR   (*shaking her*): Do you look for whippin'?

           A psalm is heard being sung below.

ABIGAIL   (*in tears*): I look for John Proctor that took me from my
           sleep and put knowledge in my heart! I never knew what
           pretence Salem was, I never knew the lying lessons I
           was taught by all these Christian women and their
           covenanted men! And now you bid me tear the light out
           of my eyes? I will not, I cannot! You loved me, John
           Proctor, and whatever sin it is, you love me yet! (*He turns
           abruptly to go out. She rushes to him.*) John, pity me, pity
           me!

           The words 'Going up to Jesus' are heard in the psalm, and
           BETTY *claps her ears suddenly and whines loudly.*

ABIGAIL   Betty? (*She hurries to Betty, who is now sitting up and
           screaming.* PROCTOR *goes to Betty as* ABIGAIL *is trying to pull
           her hands down, calling 'Betty'!*)

PROCTOR   (*growing unnerved*): What's she doing? Girl, what ails you?
           Stop that wailing!

           The singing has stopped in the midst of this, and now PARRIS
           rushes in.

PARRIS   What happened? What are you doing to her? Betty! *He
           rushes to the bed, crying, 'Betty, Betty'!* MRS PUTNAM *enters,
           feverish with curiosity, and with her* THOMAS PUTNAM *and*
           MERCY LEWIS. PARRIS, *at the bed, keeps lightly slapping Betty's
           face, while she moans and tries to get up.*

ABIGAIL   She heard you singin' and suddenly she's up and
           screamin'.

MRS PUT'M The psalm! The psalm! She cannot bear to hear the Lord's
           name!

PARRIS   No, God forbid. Mercy, run to the doctor! Tell him what's
           happened here! (MERCY LEWIS *rushes out.*)

MRS PUT'M Mark it for a sign, mark it!

REBECCA NURSE, *seventy-two, enters. She is white-haired, leaning upon her walking-stick.*

PUTNAM (*pointing at the whimpering Betty*): That is a notorious sign of witchcraft afoot, Goody Nurse, a prodigious sign!

MRS PUT'M My mother told me that! When they cannot bear to hear the name of—

PARRIS (*trembling*): Rebecca, Rebecca, go to her, we're lost. She suddenly cannot bear to hear the Lord's—

GILES COREY, *eighty-three, enters. He is knotted with muscle, canny, inquisitive, and still powerful.*

REBECCA There is hard sickness here, Giles Corey, so please to keep the quiet.

GILES I've not said a word. No one here can testify I've said a word. Is she going to fly again? I hear she flies.

PUTNAM Man, be quiet now!

Everything is quiet. REBECCA *walks across the room to the bed. Gentleness exudes from her.* BETTY *is quietly whimpering, eyes shut.* REBECCA *simply stands over the child, who gradually quiets.*

And while they are so absorbed, we may put a word in for Rebecca. Rebecca was the wife of Francis Nurse, who, from all accounts, was one of those men for whom both sides of the argument had to have respect. He was called upon to arbitrate disputes as though he were an unofficial judge, and Rebecca also enjoyed the high opinion most people had for him. By the time of the delusion, they had three hundred acres, and their children were settled in separate homesteads, within the same estate. However, Francis had originally rented the land, and one theory has it that, as he gradually paid for it and raised his social status, there were those who resented his rise.

Another suggestion to explain the systematic campaign against Rebecca, and inferentially against Francis, is the land war he fought with his neighbours, one of whom was a Putnam. This squabble grew to the proportions of a battle in the woods between partisans of both sides, and it is said to have lasted for two days. As for Rebecca herself, the general opinion of her character was so high that to explain how anyone dared cry her out for a witch–and more, how adults could bring themselves to lay hands on her–we must look to the fields and boundaries of that time.

As we have seen, Thomas Putnam's man for the Salem ministry was Bayley. The Nurse clan had been in the faction that prevented Bayley's taking office. In addition, certain families allied to the Nurses by blood or friendship, and whose farms were contiguous with the Nurse farm or close to it, combined to break away from the Salem town authority and set up Topsfield, a new and independent entity whose existence was resented by old Salemites.

That the guiding hand behind the outcry was Putnam's is indicated by the fact that, as soon as it began, this Topsfield–Nurse faction absented themselves from church in protest and disbelief. It was Edward and Jonathan Putnam who signed the first complaint against Rebecca; and Thomas Putnam's little daughter was the one who fell into a fit at the hearing and pointed to Rebecca as her attacker. To top it all, Mrs Putnam–who is now staring at the bewitched child on the bed–soon accused Rebecca's spirit of 'tempting her to iniquity', a charge that had more truth in it than Mrs Putnam could know.

MRS PUT'M (*astonished*): What have you done?

REBECCA, *in thought, now leaves the bedside and sits.*

PARRIS (*wondrous and relieved*): What do you make of it, Rebecca?

PUTNAM (*eagerly*): Goody Nurse, will you go to my Ruth and see if you can wake her?

REBECCA (*sitting*): I think she'll wake in time. Pray calm yourselves. I have eleven children, and I am twenty-six times a grandma, and I have seen them all through their silly seasons, and when it come on them they will run the Devil bowlegged keeping up with their mischief. I think she'll wake when she

tires of it. A child's spirit is like a child, you can never catch
it by running after it; you must stand still, and, for love, it
will soon itself come back.

PROCTOR   Aye, that's the truth of it, Rebecca.

MRS PUT'M   This is no silly season, Rebecca. My Ruth is bewildered,
Rebecca; she cannot eat.

REBECCA   Perhaps she is not hungered yet. (*To Parris.*) I hope you are
not decided to go in search of loose spirits, Mr Parris. I've
heard promise of that outside.

PARRIS   A wide opinion's running in the parish that the Devil may
be among us, and I would satisfy them that they are wrong.

PROCTOR   Then let you come out and call them wrong. Did you
consult the wardens before you called this minister to look
for devils?

PARRIS   He is not coming to look for devils!

PROCTOR   Then what's he coming for?

PUTNAM   There be children dyin' in the village, Mister!

PROCTOR   I seen none dyin'. This society will not be a bag to swing
around your head, Mr Putnam. (*To Parris.*) Did you call a
meeting before you–?

PUTNAM   I am sick of meetings; cannot the man turn his head without
he have a meeting?

PROCTOR   He may turn his head, but not to Hell!

REBECCA   Pray John, be calm. (*Pause. He defers to her.*) Mr Parris, I
think you'd best send Reverend Hale back as soon as he
come. This will set us all to arguin' again in the society, and
we thought to have peace this year. I think we ought rely
on the doctor now, and good prayer.

MRS PUT'M   Rebecca, the doctor's baffled!

REBECCA   If so he is, then let us go to God for the cause of it. There is
prodigious danger in the seeking of loose spirits. I fear it, I
fear it. Let us rather blame ourselves and–

PUTNAM   How may we blame ourselves? I am one of nine sons; the
Putnam seed have peopled this province. And yet I have but
one child left of eight–and now she shrivels!

REBECCA I cannot fathom that.

MRS PUT'M (*with a growing edge of sarcasm*): But I must! You think it God's work you should never lose a child, nor a grandchild either, and I bury all but one? There are wheels within wheels in this village, and fires within fires!

PUTNAM (*to Parris*): When Reverend Hale comes, you will proceed to look for signs of witchcraft here.

PROCTOR (*to Putnam*): You cannot command Mr Parris. We vote by name in this society, not by acreage.

PUTNAM I never heard you worried so on this society, Mr Proctor. I do not think I saw you at Sabbath meeting since snow flew.

PROCTOR I have trouble enough without I come five mile to hear him preach only hellfire and bloody damnation. Take it to heart, Mr Parris. There are many others who stay away from church these days because you hardly ever mention God any more.

PARRIS (*now aroused*): Why, that's a drastic charge!

REBECCA It's somewhat true; there are many that quail to bring their children–

PARRIS I do not preach for children, Rebecca. It is not the children who are unmindful of their obligations toward this ministry.

REBECCA Are there really those unmindful?

PARRIS I should say the better half of Salem village–

PUTNAM And more than that!

PARRIS Where is my wood? My contract provides I be supplied with all my firewood. I am waiting since November for a stick, and even in November I had to show my frostbitten hands like some London beggar!

GILES You are allowed six pound a year to buy your wood, Mr Parris.

PARRIS I regard that six pound as part of my salary. I am paid little enough without I spend six pound on firewood.

PROCTOR Sixty, plus six for firewood–

PARRIS   The salary is sixty-six pound, Mr Proctor! I am not some preaching farmer with a book under my arm; I am a graduate of Harvard College.

GILES   Aye, and well instructed in arithmetic!

PARRIS   Mr Corey, you will look far for a man of my kind at sixty pound a year! I am not used to this poverty; I left a thrifty business in the Barbados to serve the Lord. I do not fathom it, why am I persecuted here? I cannot offer one proposition but there be a howling riot of argument. I have often wondered if the Devil be in it somewhere; I cannot understand you people otherwise.

PROCTOR   Mr Parris, you are the first minister ever did demand the deed to this house—

PARRIS   Man! Don't a minister deserve a house to live in?

PROCTOR   To live in, yes. But to ask ownership is like you shall own the meeting house itself; the last meeting I were at you spoke so long on deeds and mortgages I thought it were an auction.

PARRIS   I want a mark of confidence, is all! I am your third preacher in seven years. I do not wish to be put out like the cat whenever some majority feels the whim. You people seem not to comprehend that a minister is the Lord's man in the parish; a minister is not to be so lightly crossed and contradicted—

PUTNAM   Aye!

PARRIS   There is either obedience or the church will burn like Hell is burning!

PROCTOR   Can you speak one minute without we land in Hell again? I am sick of Hell!

PARRIS   It is not for you to say what is good for you to hear!

PROCTOR   I may speak my heart, I think!

PARRIS   (*in a fury*): What, are we Quakers! We are not Quakers here yet, Mr Proctor. And you may tell that to your followers!

PROCTOR   My followers!

PARRIS   —(*now he's out with it*): There is a party in this church. I am not blind; there is a faction and a party.

PROCTOR   Against you?

PUTNAM   Against him and all authority!

PROCTOR   Why, then I must find it and join it.

There is a shock among the others.

REBECCA   He does not mean that.

PUTNAM   He confessed it now!

PROCTOR   I mean it solemnly, Rebecca; I like not the smell of this 'authority'.

REBECCA   No, you cannot break charity with your minister. You are another kind, John. Clasp his hand, make your peace.

PROCTOR   I have a crop to sow and lumber to drag home. (*He goes angrily to the door and turns to Corey with a smile.*) What say you, Giles, let's find the party. He says there's a party.

GILES   I've changed my opinion of this man, John. Mr Parris, I beg your pardon. I never thought you had so much iron in you.

PARRIS   (*surprised*): Why, thank you, Giles!

GILES   It suggests to the mind what the trouble be among us all these years. (*To all.*) Think on it. Wherefore is everybody suing everybody else? Think on it now, it's a deep thing, and dark as a pit. I have been six time in court this year–

PROCTOR   (*familiarly, with warmth, although he knows he is approaching the edge of Giles' tolerance with this*): Is it the Devil's fault that a man cannot say you good morning without you clap him for defamation? You're old, Giles, and you're not hearin' so well as you did.

GILES   – (*he cannot be crossed*): John Proctor, I have only last month collected four pound damages for you publicly sayin' I burned the roof off your house, and I–

PROCTOR   (*laughing*): I never said no such thing, but I've paid you for it, so I hope I can call you deaf without charge. Now come along, Giles, and help me drag my lumber home.

PUTNAM   A moment, Mr Proctor. What lumber is that you're draggin', if I may ask you?

PROCTOR   My lumber. From out my forest by the riverside.

PUTNAM   Why, we are surely gone wild this year. What anarchy is this? That tract is in my bounds, it's in my bounds, Mr Proctor.

PROCTOR In your bounds! (*Indicating Rebecca.*) I bought that tract from Goody Nurse's husband five months ago.

PUTNAM He had no right to sell it. It stands clear in my grandfather's will that all the land between the river and–

PROCTOR Your grandfather had a habit of willing land that never belonged to him, if I may say it plain.

GILES That's God's truth; he nearly willed away my north pasture but he knew I'd break his fingers before he'd set his name to it. Let's get your lumber home, John. I feel a sudden will to work coming on.

PUTNAM You load one oak of mine and you'll fight to drag it home!

GILES Aye, and we'll win too, Putnam–this fool and I. Come on! (*He turns to Proctor and starts out.*)

PUTNAM I'll have my men on you, Corey! I'll clap a writ on you!

Enter REVEREND JOHN HALE *of Beverly.*

Mr Hale is nearing forty, a tight-skinned, eager-eyed intellectual. This is a beloved errand for him; on being called here to ascertain witchcraft he felt the pride of the specialist whose unique knowledge has at last been publicly called for. Like almost all men of learning, he spent a good deal of his time pondering the invisible world, especially since he had himself encountered a witch in his parish not long before. That woman, however, turned into a mere pest under his searching scrutiny, and the child she had allegedly been afflicting recovered her normal behaviour after Hale had given her his kindness and a few days of rest in his own house. However, that experience never raised a doubt in his mind as to the reality of the underworld or the existence of Lucifer's many-faced lieutenants. And his belief is not to his discredit. Better minds than Hale's were–and still are–convinced that there is a society of spirits beyond our ken. One cannot help noting that one of his lines has never yet raised a laugh in any audience that has seen this play; it is his assurance that 'We cannot look to superstition in this. The Devil is precise.' Evidently we are not quite certain even now whether diabolism is holy and not to be scoffed at. And it is no accident that we should be so bemused.

Like Reverend Hale and the others on this stage, we conceive the Devil as a necessary part of a respectable view of cosmology. Ours is a divided empire in which certain ideas and emotions and actions are of God, and their opposites are of Lucifer. It is as impossible for most men to conceive of a morality without sin as of an earth without 'sky'. Since 1692 a great but superficial change has wiped out God's beard and the Devil's horns, but the world is still gripped between two diametrically opposed absolutes. The concept of unity, in which positive and negative are attributes of the same force, in which good and evil are relative, ever-changing, and always joined to the same phenomenon–such a concept is still reserved to the physical sciences and to the few who have grasped the history of ideas. When it is recalled that until the Christian era the underworld was never regarded as a hostile area, that all gods were useful and essentially friendly to man despite occasional lapses; when we see the steady and methodical inculcation into humanity of the idea of man's worthlessness–until redeemed– the necessity of the Devil may become evident as a weapon, a weapon designed and used time and time again in every age to whip men into a surrender to a particular church or church-state.

Our difficulty in believing the–for want of a better word–political inspiration of the Devil is due in great part to the fact that he is called up and damned not only by our social antagonists but by our own side, whatever it may be. The Catholic Church, through its Inquisition, is famous for cultivating Lucifer as the arch-fiend, but the Church's enemies relied no less upon the Old Boy to keep the human mind enthralled. Luther was himself accused of alliance with Hell, and he in turn accused his enemies. To complicate matters further, he believed that he had had contact with the Devil and had argued theology with him. I am not surprised at this, for at my own university a professor of history–a Lutheran, by the way–used to assemble his graduate students, draw the shades, and commune in the classroom with Erasmus. He was never, to my knowledge, officially scoffed at for this, the reason being that the university officials, like most of us, are the children of a history which still sucks at the Devil's teats. At this writing, only England has held back before the temptations of contemporary diabolism. In the countries of the Communist ideology, all resistance of any import is linked to the totally malign capitalist succubi, and in America any man who is not reactionary in his views is open to the charge of alliance with the Red hell. Political opposition, thereby, is given an inhumane overlay which then justifies the abrogation of all normally applied customs of civilized intercourse. A political policy is equated with moral right, and opposition to it with diabolical malevolence. Once such an equation is effectively made, society becomes a congerie of plots and counterplots, and the main role of government changes from that of the arbiter to that of the scourge of God.

The results of this process are no different now from what they ever were, except sometimes in the degree of cruelty inflicted, and not always even in that depart-ment. Normally the actions and deeds of a man were all that society felt comfortable in judging. The secret intent of an action was left to the ministers, priests, and rabbis to deal with. When diabolism rises, however, actions are the least important manifests of the true nature of a man. The Devil, as Reverend Hale said, is a wily one, and, until an hour before he fell, even God thought him beautiful in Heaven.

The analogy, however, seems to falter when one considers that, while there were no witches then, there are Communists and capitalists now, and in each camp there is certain proof that spies of each side are at work undermining the other. But this is a snobbish objection and not at all warranted by the facts. I have no doubt that people *were* communing with, and even worshipping, the Devil in Salem, and if the whole truth could be known in this case, as it is in others, we should discover a regular and conventionalized propitiation of the dark spirit. One certain evidence of this is the confession of Tituba, the slave of Reverend Parris, and another is the behaviour of the children who were known to have indulged in sorceries with her.

There are accounts of similar *klatches* in Europe, where the daughters of the towns would assemble at night and, sometimes with fetishes, sometimes with a selected young man, give themselves to love, with some bastardly results. The Church, sharp-eyed, as it must be when gods long dead are brought to life, condemned these orgies as witchcraft and interpreted them, rightly, as a resurgence of the Dionysiac forces it had crushed long before. Sex, sin, and the Devil were early linked, and so they continued to be in Salem, and are today. From all accounts there are no more puritanical mores in the world than those enforced by the Communists in Russia, where women's fashions, for instance, are as prudent and all-covering as any American Baptist would desire. The divorce laws lay a tremendous responsibility on the father for the care of his children. Even the laxity of divorce regulations in the early years of the revolution was undoubtedly a revulsion from the nineteenth-century Victorian immobility of marriage and the consequent hypocrisy that developed from it. If for no other reasons, a state so powerful, so jealous of the uniformity of its citizens, cannot long tolerate the atomization of the family. And yet, in American eyes at least, there remains the conviction that the Russian attitude toward women is lascivious. It is the Devil working again, just as he is working within the Slav who is shocked at the very idea of a woman's disrobing herself in a burlesque show. Our opposites are always robed in sexual sin, and it is from this unconscious conviction that demonology gains both its attractive sensuality and its capacity to infuriate and frighten.

Coming into Salem now, Reverend Hale conceives of himself

much as a young doctor on his first call. His painfully acquired armoury of symptoms, catchwords, and diagnostic procedures are now to be put to use at last. The road from Beverly is unusually busy this morning, and he has passed a hundred rumours that make him smile at the ignorance of the yeomanry in this most precise science. He feels himself allied with the best minds of Europe–kings, philosophers, scientists, and ecclesiasts of all churches. His goal, is light, goodness and its preservation, and he knows the exaltation of the blessed whose intelligence, sharpened by minute examinations of enormous tracts, is finally called upon to face what may be a bloody fight with the Fiend himself.

He appears loaded down with half a dozen heavy books.

HALE   Pray you, someone take these!

PARRIS   (*delighted*): Mr Hale! Oh! it's good to see you again! (*Taking some books.*): My, they're heavy!

HALE   (*setting down his books*) They must be; they are weighted with authority.

PARRIS   (*a little scared*): Well, you do come prepared!

HALE   We shall need hard study if it comes to tracking down the Old Boy. (*Noticing Rebecca.*) You cannot be Rebecca Nurse?

REBECCA I am, sir. Do you know me?

HALE   It's strange how I knew you, but I suppose you look as such a good soul should. We have all heard of your great charities in Beverly.

PARRIS   Do you know this gentleman? Mr Thomas Putnam. And his good wife Ann.

HALE   Putnam! I had not expected such distinguished company, sir.

PUTNAM   (*pleased*): It does not seem to help us today, Mr Hale. We look to you to come to our house and save our child.

HALE   Your child ails too?

MRS PUT'M Her soul, her soul seems flown away. She sleeps and yet she walks . . .

PUTNAM   She cannot eat.

HALE	Cannot eat! (*Thinks on it. Then, to Proctor and Giles Corey.*) Do you men have afflicted children?
PARRIS	No, no, these are farmers. John Proctor–
GILES	He don't believe in witches.
PROCTOR	(*to Hale*): I never spoke on witches one way or the other. Will you come, Giles?
GILES	No–no, John, I think not. I have some few queer questions of my own to ask this fellow.
PROCTOR	I've heard you to be a sensible man, Mr Hale. I hope you'll leave some of it in Salem.

PROCTOR *goes.* HALE *stands embarrassed for an instant.*

PARRIS	(*quickly*): Will you look at my daughter, sir? (*Leads Hale to the bed.*) She has tried to leap out the window; we discovered her this morning on the highroad, waving her arms as though she'd fly.
HALE	(*narrowing his eyes*): Tries to fly.
PUTNAM	She cannot bear to hear the Lord's name, Mr Hale; that's a sure sign of witchcraft afloat.
HALE	(*holding up his hands*): No, no. Now let me instruct you. We cannot look to superstition in this. The Devil is precise; the marks of his presence are definite as stone, and I must tell you all that I shall not proceed unless you are prepared to believe me if I should find no bruise of hell upon her.
PARRIS	It is agreed, sir–it is agreed–we will abide by your judgement.
HALE	Good then. (*He goes to the bed, looks down at Betty. To Parris.*) Now, sir, what were your first warning of this strangeness?
PARRIS	Why, sir–I discovered her–(*indicating Abigail*)–and my niece and ten or twelve of the other girls, dancing in the forest last night.
HALE	(*surprised*): You permit dancing?
PARRIS	No, no, it were secret–
MRS PUT'M	(*unable to wait*): Mr Parris's slave has knowledge of conjurin', sir.
PARRIS	(*to Mrs Putnam*): We cannot be sure of that, Goody Ann–

MRS PUT'M (*frightened, very softly*): I know it, sir. I sent my child–she
should learn from Tituba who murdered her sisters.

REBECCA (*horrified*): Goody Ann! You sent a child to conjure up the
dead?

MRS PUT'M Let God blame me, not you, not you, Rebecca! I'll not have
you judging me any more! (*To Hale.*) Is it a natural work to
lose seven children before they live a day?

PARRIS Sssh!

REBECCA, *with great pain, turns her face away. There is a pause.*

HALE Seven dead in childbirth.

MRS PUT'M (*softly*): Aye. (*Her voice breaks; she looks up at him. Silence.
HALE is impressed. PARRIS looks to him. He goes to his books,
opens one, turns pages, then reads. All wait, avidly.*)

PARRIS (*hushed*): What book is that?

MRS PUT'M What's there, sir?

HALE (*with a tasty love of intellectual pursuit*): Here is all the
invisible world, caught, defined, and calculated. In these
books the Devil stands stripped of all his brute disguises. Here
are all your familiar spirits–your incubi and succubi; your
witches that go by land, by air, and by sea; your wizards of
the night and of the day. Have no fear now–we shall find him
out if he has come among us, and I mean to crush him utterly
if he has shown his face! (*He starts for the bed.*)

REBECCA Will it hurt the child, sir?

HALE I cannot tell. If she is truly in the Devil's grip we may have
to rip and tear to get her free.

REBECCA I think I'll go, then. I am too old for this. (*She rises.*)

PARRIS (*striving for conviction*): Why, Rebecca, we may open up the
boil of all our troubles today!

REBECCA Let us hope for that. I go to God for you, sir.

PARRIS (*with trepidation–and resentment*): I hope you do not mean
we go to Satan here! (*Slight pause.*)

REBECCA I wish I knew. (*She goes out; they feel resentful of her note of
moral superiority.*)

PUTNAM (*abruptly*): Come, Mr Hale, let's get on. Sit you here.

GILES   Mr Hale, I have always wanted to ask a learned man—what signifies the readin' of strange books?

HALE   What books?

GILES   I cannot tell; she hides them.

HALE   Who does this?

GILES   Martha, my wife. I have waked at night many a time and found her in a corner, readin' of a book. Now what do you make of that?

HALE   Why, that's not necessarily—

GILES   It discomforts me! Last night—mark this—I tried and tried and could not say my prayers. And then she close her book and walks out of the house, and suddenly—mark this—I could pray again!

Old Giles must be spoken for, if only because his fate was to be so remarkable and so different from that of all the others. He was in his early eighties at this time, and was the most comical hero in the history. No man has ever been blamed for so much. If a cow was missed, the first thought was to look for her around Corey's house; a fire blazing up at night brought suspicion of arson to his door. He didn't give a hoot for public opinion, and only in his last years—after he had married Martha— did he bother much with the church. That she stopped his prayer is very probable, but he forgot to say that he'd only recently learned any prayers and it didn't take much to make him stumble over them. He was a crank and a nuisance, but withal a deeply innocent and brave man. In court, once, he was asked if it were true that he had been frightened by the strange behaviour of a hog and had then said he knew it to be the Devil in an animal's shape. 'What frighted you?' he was asked. He forgot everything but the word 'frighted', and instantly replied 'I do not know that I ever spoke that word in my life.'

HALE   Ah! the stoppage of prayer—that is strange. I'll speak further on that with you.

GILES   I'm not sayin' she's touched the Devil, now, but I'd admire to know what books she reads and why she hides them. She'll not answer me, y'see.

HALE   Aye, we'll discuss it. (*To all.*) Now mark me, if the Devil is in her you will witness some frightful wonders in this room, so please to keep your wits about you. Mr Putnam, stand close in case she flies. Now, Betty, dear, will you sit up? (PUTNAM *comes in closer, ready-handed.* HALE *sits Betty up, but she hangs limp in his hands.*) Hmmm. (*He observes her carefully. The others watch breathlessly.*) Can you hear me? I am John Hale, minister of Beverly, I have come to help you, dear. Do you remember my two little girls in Beverly? (*She does not stir in his hands.*)

PARRIS   (*in fright*): How can it be the Devil? Why would he choose my house to strike? We have all manner of licentious people in the village!

HALE   What victory would the Devil have to win a soul already bad? It is the best the Devil wants, and who is better than the minister?

GILES   That's deep, Mr Parris, deep, deep!

PARRIS   (*with resolution now*): Betty! Answer Mr Hale! Betty!

HALE   Does someone afflict you, child? It need not be a woman, mind you, or a man. Perhaps some bird invisible to others comes to you–perhaps a pig, a mouse, or any beast at all. Is there some figure bids you fly? (*The child remains limp in his hands. In silence he lays her back on the pillow. Now, holding out his hands toward her, he intones.*) In nomine Domini Sabaoth sui filiique ite ad infernos. (*She does not stir. He turns to Abigail, his eyes narrowing.*) Abigail, what sort of dancing were you doing with her in the forest?

ABIGAIL   Why–common dancing is all.

PARRIS   I think I ought to say that I–I saw a kettle in the grass where they were dancing.

ABIGAIL   That were only soup.

HALE   What sort of soup were in this kettle, Abigail?

ABIGAIL	Why, it were beans–and lentils, I think, and–
HALE	Mr Parris, you did not notice, did you, any living thing in the kettle? A mouse, perhaps, a spider, a frog–?
PARRIS	(*fearfully*): I–do believe there were some movement–in the soup.
ABIGAIL	That jumped in, we never put it in!
HALE	(*quickly*): What jumped in?
ABIGAIL	Why a very little frog jumped–
PARRIS	A frog, Abby?
HALE	(*grasping Abigail*): Abigail, it may be your cousin is dying. Did you call the Devil last night?
ABIGAIL	I never called him! Tituba, Tituba . . .
PARRIS	(*blanched*): She called the Devil?
HALE	I should like to speak with Tituba.
PARRIS	Goody Ann, will you bring her up? (*Mrs Putnam exits.*)
HALE	How did she call him?
ABIGAIL	I know not–she spoke Barbados.
HALE	Did you feel any strangeness when she called him? A sudden cold wind, perhaps? A trembling below the ground?
ABIGAIL	I didn't see no Devil! (*Shaking Betty.*) Betty, wake up. Betty! Betty!
HALE	You cannot evade me, Abigail. Did your cousin drink any of the brew in that kettle?
ABIGAIL	She never drank it!
HALE	Did you drink it?
ABIGAIL	No, sir!
HALE	Did Tituba ask you to drink it?
ABIGAIL	She tried but I refused.
HALE	Why are you concealing? Have you sold yourself to Lucifer?
ABIGAIL	I never sold myself! I'm a good girl! I'm a proper girl! MRS PUTNAM *enters with* TITUBA *and instantly* ABIGAIL *points at Tituba.*
ABIGAIL	She made me do it! She made Betty do it!
TITUBA	(*shocked and angry*): Abby!

ABIGAIL She makes me drink blood!

PARRIS Blood!!

MRS PUT'M My baby's blood?

TITUBA No, no, chicken blood. I give she chicken blood!

HALE Woman, have you enlisted these children for the Devil?

TITUBA No, no, sir, I don't truck with no Devil!

HALE Why can she not wake? Are you silencing this child?

TITUBA I love me Betty!

HALE You have sent your spirit out upon this child, have you not? Are you gathering souls for the Devil?

ABIGAIL She sends her spirit on me in church; she makes me laugh at prayer!

PARRIS She have often laughed at prayer!

ABIGAIL She comes to me every night to go and drink blood!

TITUBA You beg *me* to conjure! She beg *me* make charm –

ABIGAIL Don't lie! (*To Hale.*) She comes to me while I sleep; she's always making me dream corruptions!

TITUBA Why you say that, Abby?

ABIGAIL Sometimes I wake and find myself standing in the open doorway and not a stitch on my body! I always hear her laughing in my sleep. I hear her singing her Barbados songs and tempting me with–

TITUBA Mister Reverend, I never –

HALE (*resolved now*): Tituba, I want you to wake this child.

TITUBA I have no power on this child, sir.

HALE You most certainly do, and you will free her from it now! When did you compact with the Devil?

TITUBA I don't compact with no Devil!

PARRIS You will confess yourself or I will take you out and whip you to your death, Tituba!

PUTNAM This woman must be hanged! She must be taken and hanged!

TITUBA (*terrified, falls to her knees*): No, no, don't hang Tituba! I tell him I don't desire to work for him, sir.

PARRIS The Devil?

HALE	Then you saw him! (*Tituba weeps.*) Now Tituba, I know that when we bind ourselves to Hell it is very hard to break with it. We are going to help you tear yourself free –
TITUBA	(*frightened by the coming process*): Mister Reverend, I do believe somebody else be witchin' these children.
HALE	Who?
TITUBA	I don't know, sir, but the Devil got him numerous witches.
HALE	Does he! (*It is a clue.*) Tituba, look into my eyes. Come look into me. (*She raises her eyes to his fearfully.*) You would be a good Christian woman, would you not, Tituba?
TITUBA	Aye, sir, a good Christian woman.
HALE	And you love these little children?
TITUBA	Oh, yes, sir, I don't desire to hurt little children.
HALE	And you love God, Tituba?
TITUBA	I love God with all my bein'.
HALE	Now, in God's holy name–
TITUBA	Bless Him. Bless Him. (*She is rocking on her knees, sobbing in terror.*)
HALE	And to His glory –
TITUBA	Eternal glory. Bless Him – bless God . . .
HALE	Open yourself, Tituba – open yourself and let God's holy light shine on you.
TITUBA	Oh, bless the Lord.
HALE	When the Devil comes to you does he ever come–with another person? (*She stares up into his face.*) Perhaps another person in the village? Someone you know.
PARRIS	Who came with him?
PUTNAM	Sarah Good? Did you ever see Sarah Good with him? Or Osburn?
PARRIS	Was it man or woman came with him?
TITUBA	Man or woman. Was – was woman.
PARRIS	What woman? A woman, you said. What woman?
TITUBA	It was black dark, and I –
PARRIS	You could see him. Why could you not see her?

TITUBA Well, they was always talking; they was always runnin'
round and carryin' on –

PARRIS You mean out of Salem? Salem witches?

TITUBA I believe so, yes, sir.

Now HALE *takes her hand. She is surprised.*

HALE Tituba. You must have no fear to tell us who they are, do
you understand? We will protect you. The Devil can never
overcome a minister. You know that, do you not?

TITUBA (*kisses Hale's hand*): Aye, sir, oh, I do.

HALE You have confessed yourself to witchcraft, and that speaks a
wish to come to Heaven's side. And we will bless you,
Tituba.

TITUBA (*deeply relieved*): Oh, God bless you, Mr Hale!

HALE (*with rising exaltation*): You are God's instrument put in our
hands to discover the Devil's agents among us. You are
selected, Tituba, turn your back on him and face God – face
God, Tituba, and God will protect you.

TITUBA (*joining with him*): Oh, God, protect Tituba!

HALE (*kindly*): Who came to you with the Devil? Two? Three?
Four? How many?

TITUBA *pants, and begins rocking back and forth again,
staring ahead.*

TITUBA There was four. There was four.

PARRIS (*pressing in on her*): Who? Who? Their names, their
names!

TITUBA (*suddenly bursting out*): Oh, how many times he bid me kill
you, Mr Parris!

PARRIS Kill me!

TITUBA (*in a fury*): He say Mr Parris must be kill! Mr Parris no goodly
man, Mr Parris mean man and no gentle man, and he bid me
rise out of my bed and cut your throat! (*They gasp.*) But I tell
him 'No! I don't hate that man. I don't want kill that man.'
But he say, 'You work for me, Tituba, and I make you free! I
give you pretty dress to wear, and put you way high up

in the air, and you gone fly back to Barbados!' And I say 'You lie, Devil, you lie!' And then he come one stormy night to me, and he say, 'Look! I have white people belong to me.' And I look—and there was Goody Good.

PARRIS   Sarah Good.

TITUBA   (*rocking and weeping*): Aye, sir, and Goody Osburn.

MRS PUT'M   I knew it! Goody Osburn were midwife to me three times. I begged you, Thomas, did I not? I begged him not to call Osburn because I feared her. My babies always shrivelled in her hands!

HALE   Take courage, you must give us all their names. How can you bear to see this child suffering? Look at her, Tituba. (*He is indicating Betty on the bed.*) Look at her God-given innocence; her soul is so tender; we must protect her, Tituba; the Devil is out and preying on her like a beast upon the flesh of the pure lamb. God will bless you for your help.

ABIGAIL *rises, staring as though inspired, and cries out.*

ABIGAIL   I want to open myself! (*They turn to her, startled. She is enraptured, as though in a pearly light.*) I want the light of God, I want the sweet love of Jesus! I danced for the Devil; I saw him; I wrote in his book; I go back to Jesus; I kiss His hand. I saw Sarah Good with the Devil! I saw Goody Osburn with the Devil! I saw Bridget Bishop with the Devil!

As she is speaking, BETTY *is rising from the bed, a fever in her eyes, and picks up the chant.*

BETTY   (*staring too*): I saw George Jacobs with the Devil! I saw Goody Howe with the Devil!

PARRIS   She speaks! (*He rushes to embrace Betty.*) She speaks!

HALE   Glory to God! It is broken, they are free!

BETTY   (*calling out hysterically and with great relief*): I saw Martha Bellows with the Devil!

ABIGAIL   I saw Goody Sibber with the Devil! (*It is rising to a great glee.*)

PUTNAM   The marshal, I'll call the marshal!

PARRIS *is shouting a prayer of thanksgiving.*

BETTY I saw Alice Barrow with the Devil!

The curtain begins to fall.

HALE (*as Putnam goes out*): Let the marshal bring irons!

ABIGAIL I saw Goody Hawkins with the Devil!

BETTY I saw Goody Bibber with the Devil!

ABIGAIL I saw Goody Booth with the Devil!

On their ecstatic cries

THE CURTAIN FALLS

ACT TWO

The common room of Proctor's house, eight days later.

At the right is a door opening on the fields outside. A fireplace is at the left, and behind it a stairway leading upstairs. It is the low, dark, and rather long living room of the time. As the curtain rises, the room is empty. From above, Elizabeth is heard softly singing to the children. Presently the door opens and JOHN PROCTOR *enters, carrying his gun. He glances about the room as he comes toward the fireplace, then halts for an instant as he hears her singing. He continues on to the fireplace, leans the gun against the wall as he swings a pot out of the fire and smells it. Then he lifts out the ladle and tastes. He is not quite pleased. He reaches to a cupboard, takes a pinch of salt, and drops it into the pot. As he is tasting again, her footsteps are heard on the stair. He swings the pot into the fireplace and goes to a basin and washes his hands and face.* ELIZABETH *enters.*

ELIZABETH What keeps you so late? It's almost dark.

PROCTOR I were planting far out to the forest edge.

ELIZABETH Oh, you're done then.

PROCTOR Aye, the farm is seeded. The boys asleep?

ELIZABETH They will be soon. (*And she goes to the fireplace and proceeds to ladle up a stew in a dish.*)

PROCTOR Pray now for a fair summer.

ELIZABETH Aye.

PROCTOR Are you well today?

ELIZABETH I am. (*She brings the plate to the table, and, indicating the food.*) It is a rabbit.

PROCTOR (*going to the table*): Oh, is it! In Jonathan's trap?

ELIZABETH No, she walked into the house this afternoon; found her sittin' in the corner like she come to visit.

PROCTOR Oh, that's a good sign walkin' in.

ELIZABETH Pray God. I hurt my heart to strip her, poor rabbit.
She sits and watches him taste it.

PROCTOR   It's well seasoned.

ELIZABETH (*blushing with pleasure*): I took great care. She's tender?

PROCTOR   Aye. (*He eats. She watches him.*) I think we'll see green
           fields soon. It's warm as blood beneath the clods.

ELIZABETH That's well.

           PROCTOR *eats, then looks up.*

PROCTOR   If the crop is good I'll buy George Jacob's heifer. How
           would that please you?

ELIZABETH Aye, it would.

PROCTOR   (*with a grin*): I mean to please you, Elizabeth.

ELIZABETH – (*it is hard to say*): I know it, John.

           *He gets up, goes to her, kisses her. She receives it. With a
           certain disappointment, he returns to the table.*

PROCTOR   (*as gently as he can*): Cider?

ELIZABETH (*with a sense of reprimanding herself for having forgot*):
           Aye! (*She gets up and goes and pours a glass for him. He
           now arches his back.*)

PROCTOR   This farm's a continent when you go foot by foot droppin'
           seeds in it.

ELIZABETH (*coming with the cider*): It must be.

PROCTOR   (*drinks a long draught, then, putting the glass down*): You
           ought to bring some flowers in the house.

ELIZABETH Oh! I forgot! I will tomorrow.

PROCTOR   It's winter in here yet. On Sunday let you come with me,
           and we'll walk the farm together; I never see such a load
           of flowers on the earth. (*With good feeling he goes and
           looks up at the sky through the open doorway.*) Lilacs have
           a purple smell. Lilac is the smell of nightfall, I think.
           Massachusetts is a beauty in the spring!

ELIZABETH Aye, it is.

           *There is a pause. She is watching him from the table as he
           stands there absorbing the night. It is as though she would
           speak but cannot. Instead, now, she takes up his plate and
           glass and fork and goes with them to the basin. Her back is
           turned to him. He turns to her and watches her. A sense of
           their separation arises.*

PROCTOR	I think you're sad again. Are you?
ELIZABETH	– (*She doesn't want friction, and yet she must*): You come so late I thought you'd gone to Salem this afternoon.
PROCTOR	Why! I have no business in Salem.
ELIZABETH	You did speak of going, earlier this week.
PROCTOR	– (*he knows what she means*): I thought better of it since.
ELIZABETH	Mary Warren's there today.
PROCTOR	Why'd you let her? You heard me forbid her go to Salem any more!
ELIZABETH	I couldn't stop her.
PROCTOR	(*holding back a full condemnation of her*): It is a fault, it is a fault Elizabeth – you're the mistress here, not Mary Warren.
ELIZABETH	She frightened all my strength away.
PROCTOR	How may that mouse frighten you, Elizabeth? You –
ELIZABETH	It is a mouse no more. I forbid her go, and she raises up her chin like the daughter of a prince and says to me, 'I must go to Salem, Goody Proctor; I am an official of the court!'
PROCTOR	Court! What court?
ELIZABETH	Aye, it is a proper court they have now. They've sent four judges out of Boston, she says, weighty magistrates of the General Court, and at the head sits the Deputy Governor of the Province.
PROCTOR	(*astonished*): Why, she's mad.
ELIZABETH	I would to God she were. There be fourteen people in the jail now, she says. (PROCTOR *simply looks at her, unable to grasp it.*) And they'll be tried, and the court have power to hang them too, she says.
PROCTOR	(*scoffing, but without conviction*): Ah, they'd never hang –
ELIZABETH	The Deputy Governor promise hangin' if they'll not confess, John. The town's gone wild, I think. She speak of Abigail, and I thought she were a saint, to hear her. Abigail brings the other girls into the court, and where she walks the crowd will part like the sea for Israel. And folk are brought

before them, and if they scream and howl and fall to the floor – the person's clapped in the jail for bewitchin' them.

PROCTOR (*wide-eyed*): Oh, it is a black mischief.

ELIZABETH I think you must go to Salem, John. (*He turns to her.*) I think so. You must tell them it is a fraud.

PROCTOR (*thinking beyond this*): Aye, it is, it is surely.

ELIZABETH Let you go to Ezekiel Cheever – he knows you well. And tell him what she said to you last week in her uncle's house. She said it had naught to do with witchcraft, did she not?

PROCTOR (*in thought*): Aye, she did, she did. (*Now a pause.*)

ELIZABETH (*quietly, fearing to anger him by prodding*): God forbid you keep that from the court, John. I think they must be told.

PROCTOR (*quietly, struggling with his thought*): Ay, they must, they must. It is a wonder they do believe her.

ELIZABETH I would go to Salem now, John – let you go tonight.

PROCTOR I'll think on it.

ELIZABETH (*with her courage now*): You cannot keep it, John.

PROCTOR (*angering*): I know I cannot keep it. I say I will think on it!

ELIZABETH (*hurt, and very coldly*): Good, then, let you think on it. (*She stands and starts to walk out of the room.*)

PROCTOR I am only wondering how I may prove what she told me, Elizabeth. If the girl's a saint now, I think it is not easy to prove she's fraud, and the town gone so silly. She told it to me in a room alone – I have no proof for it.

ELIZABETH You were alone with her?

PROCTOR (*stubbornly*): For a moment alone, aye.

ELIZABETH Why, then, it is not as you told me.

PROCTOR (*his anger rising*): For a moment, I say. The others come in soon after.

ELIZABETH (*quietly – she has suddenly lost all faith in him*): Do as you wish, then. (*She starts to turn.*)

PROCTOR Woman. (*She turns to him.*) I'll not have your suspicion any more.

ELIZABETH	(*a little loftily*): I have no –
PROCTOR	I'll not have it!
ELIZABETH	Then let you not earn it.
PROCTOR	(*with a violent undertone*): You doubt me yet?
ELIZABETH	(*with a smile, to keep her dignity*): John, if it were not Abigail that you must go to hurt, would you falter now? I think not.
PROCTOR	Now look you –
ELIZABETH	I see what I see, John.
PROCTOR	(*with solemn warning*): You will not judge me more, Elizabeth. I have good reason to think before I charge fraud on Abigail, and I will think on it. Let you look to your own improvement before you go to judge your husband any more. I have forgot Abigail, and –
ELIZABETH	And I.
PROCTOR	Spare me! You forget nothin' and forgive nothin'. Learn charity, woman. I have gone tiptoe in this house all seven month since she is gone. I have not moved from there to there without I think to please you, and still an everlasting funeral marches round your heart. I cannot speak but I am doubted, every moment judged for lies, as though I come into a court when I come into this house!
ELIZABETH	John, you are not open with me. You saw her with a crowd, you said. Now you –
PROCTOR	I'll plead my honesty no more, Elizabeth.
ELIZABETH	– (*now she would justify herself*): John, I am only –
PROCTOR	No more! I should have roared you down when first you told me your suspicion. But I wilted, and, like a Christian, I confessed. Confessed! Some dream I had must have mistaken you for God that day. But you're not, you're not, and let you remember it! Let you look sometimes for the goodness in me, and judge me not.
ELIZABETH	I do not judge you. The magistrate sits in your heart that judges you. I never thought you but a good man, John – (*with a smile*) – only somewhat bewildered.

PROCTOR (*laughing bitterly*); Oh, Elizabeth, your justice would freeze beer! (*He turns suddenly towards a sound outside. He starts for the door as* MARY WARREN *enters. As soon as he sees her, he goes directly to her and grabs her by her cloak, furious*). How do you go to Salem when I forbid it? Do you mock me? (*Shaking her.*) I'll whip you if you dare leave this house again!

Strangely, she doesn't resist him, but hangs limply by his grip.

MARY I am sick, I am sick, Mr Proctor. Pray, pray, hurt me not. (*Her strangeness throws him off, and her evident pallor and weakness. He frees her.*) My insides are all shuddery; I am in the proceedings all day, sir.

PROCTOR (*with draining anger–his curiosity is draining it*): And what of these proceedings here? When will you proceed to keep this house, as you are paid nine pound a year to do–and my wife not wholly well?

As though to compensate, MARY WARREN *goes to Elizabeth with a small rag doll.*

MARY I made a gift for you today, Goody Proctor. I had to sit long hours in a chair, and passed the time with sewing.

ELIZABETH (*perplexed, looking at the doll*): Why, thank you, it's a fair poppet.

MARY (*with a trembling, decayed voice*): We must all love each other now, Goody Proctor.

ELIZABETH (*amazed at her strangeness*): Aye, indeed we must.

MARY (*glancing at the room*): I'll get up early in the morning and clean the house. I must sleep now. (*She turns and starts off.*)

PROCTOR Mary. (*She halts.*) Is it true? There be fourteen women arrested?

MARY No, sir. There be thirty-nine now – (*She suddenly breaks off and sobs and sits down, exhausted.*)

ELIZABETH Why, she's weepin'! What ails you, child?

MARY Goody Osburn – will hang!

There is a shocked pause, while she sobs.

PROCTOR Hang! (*He calls into her face.*) Hang, y'say?

MARY	(*through her weeping*): Aye.
PROCTOR	The Deputy Governor will permit it?
MARY	He sentenced her. He must. (*To ameliorate it.*) But not Sarah Good. For Sarah Good confessed, y'see.
PROCTOR	Confessed! To what?
MARY	That she – (*in horror at the memory*) – she sometimes made a compact with Lucifer, and wrote her name in his black book – with her blood – and bound herself to torment Christians till God's thrown down – and we all must worship Hell forevermore.
	Pause.
PROCTOR	But – surely you know what a jabberer she is. Did you tell them that?
MARY	Mr Proctor, in open court she near to choked us all to death.
PROCTOR	How, choked you?
MARY	She sent her spirit out.
ELIZABETH	Oh, Mary, Mary, surely you –
MARY	(*with an indignant edge*): She tried to kill me many times, Goody Proctor!
ELIZABETH	Why, I never heard you mention that before.
MARY	I never knew it before. I never knew anything before. When she came into the court I say to myself, I must not accuse this woman, for she sleep in ditches, and so very old and poor. But then – then she sit there, denying and denying, and I feel a misty coldness climbin' up my back, and the skin on my skull begin to creep, and I feel a clamp around my neck and I cannot breathe air; and then – (*entranced*) – I hear a voice, a screamin' voice, and it were my voice – and all at once I remembered everything she done to me!
PROCTOR	Why? What did she do to you?
MARY	(*like one awakened to a marvellous secret insight*): So many time, Mr Proctor, she come to this very door, beggin'

bread and a cup of cider – and mark this: whenever I turned her away empty, she *mumbled.*

ELIZABETH Mumbled! She may mumble if she's hungry.

MARY But *what* does she mumble? You must remember, Goody Proctor. Last month – a Monday, I think – she walked away, and I thought my guts would burst for two days after. Do you remember it?

ELIZABETH Why – I do, I think, but –

MARY And so I told that to Judge Hathorne, and he asks her so. 'Goody Osburn,' says he, 'what curse do you mumble that this girl must fall sick after turning you away?' And she replies – (*mimicking an old crone*) – 'Why, your excellence, no curse at all. I only say my commandments; I hope I may say my commandments,' says she!

ELIZABETH And that's an upright answer.

MARY Aye, but then Judge Hathorne say, 'Recite for us your commandments!' – (*leaning avidly toward them*) – and of all the ten she could not say a single one. She never knew no commandments, and they had her in a flat lie!

PROCTOR And so condemned her?

MARY (*now a little strained, seeing his stubborn doubt*): Why, they must when she condemned herself.

PROCTOR But the proof, the proof!

MARY (*with greater impatience with him*): I told you the proof. It's hard proof, hard as rock, the judges said.

PROCTOR (*pauses an instant, then*): You will not go to court again, Mary Warren.

MARY I must tell you, sir, I will be gone every day now. I am amazed you do not see what weighty work we do.

PROCTOR What work you do! It's strange work for a Christian girl to hang old women!

MARY But, Mr Proctor, they will not hang them if they confess. Sarah Good will only sit in jail some time – (*recalling*) – and here's a wonder for you; think on this. Goody Good is pregnant!

ELIZABETH   Pregnant! Are they mad? The woman's near to sixty!

MARY   They had Doctor Griggs examine her, and she's full to the brim. And smokin' a pipe all these years, and no husband either! But she's safe, thank God, for they'll not hurt the innocent child. But be that not a marvel? You must see it, sir, it's God's work we do. So I'll be gone every day for some time. I'm – I am an official of the court, they say, and I – (*She has been edging toward offstage.*)

PROCTOR   I'll official you! (*He strides to the mantel, takes down the whip hanging there.*)

MARY   (*terrified, but coming erect, striving for her authority*): I'll not stand whipping any more!

ELIZABETH   (*hurriedly, as Proctor approaches*): Mary, promise now you'll stay at home –

MARY   (*backing from him, but keeping her erect posture, striving, striving for her way*): The Devil's loose in Salem, Mr Proctor; we must discover where he's hiding!

PROCTOR   I'll whip the Devil out of you! (*With whip raised he reaches out for her, and she streaks away and yells.*)

MARY   (*pointing at Elizabeth*): I saved her life today!

Silence. His whip comes down.

ELIZABETH   (*softly*): I am accused?

MARY   (*quaking*): Somewhat mentioned. But I said I never see no sign you ever sent your spirit out to hurt no one, and seeing I do live so closely with you, they dismissed it.

ELIZABETH   Who accused me?

MARY   I am bound by law, I cannot tell it. (*To Proctor.*) I only hope you'll not be so sarcastical no more. Four judges and the King's deputy sat to dinner with us but an hour ago. I – I would have you speak civilly to me, from this out.

PROCTOR   (*in horror, muttering in disgust at her*): Go to bed.

MARY   (*with a stamp of her foot*): I'll not be ordered to bed no more, Mr Proctor! I am eighteen and a woman, however single!

PROCTOR   Do you wish to sit up? Then sit up.

MARY	I wish to go to bed!
PROCTOR	(*in anger*): Good night, then!
MARY	Good night. (*Dissatisfied, uncertain of herself, she goes out. Wide-eyed, both* PROCTOR *and* ELIZABETH *stand staring.*)
ELIZABETH	(*quietly*): Oh, the noose, the noose is up!
PROCTOR	There'll be no noose.
ELIZABETH	She wants me dead. I knew all week it would come to this!
PROCTOR	(*without conviction*): They dismissed it. You heard her say –
ELIZABETH	And what of tomorrow? She will cry me out until they take me!
PROCTOR	Sit you down.
ELIZABETH	She wants me dead, John, you know it!
PROCTOR	I say sit down! (*She sits, trembling. He speaks quietly, trying to keep his wits.*) Now we must be wise, Elizabeth.
ELIZABETH	(*with sarcasm, and a sense of being lost*): Oh, indeed, indeed!
PROCTOR	Fear nothing. I'll find Ezekiel Cheever. I'll tell him she said it were all sport.
ELIZABETH	John, with so many in the jail, more than Cheever's help is needed now, I think. Would you favour me with this? Go to Abigail.
PROCTOR	(*his soul hardening as he senses . . .*): What have I to say to Abigail?
ELIZABETH	(*delicately*): John – grant me this. You have a faulty understanding of young girls. There is a promise made in any bed –
PROCTOR	(*striving against his anger*): What promise!
ELIZABETH	Spoke or silent, a promise is surely made. And she may dote on it now – I am sure she does – and thinks to kill me, then to take my place.
	Proctor's anger is rising; he cannot speak.
ELIZABETH	It is her dearest hope, John, I know it. There be a thousand

names; why does she call mine? There be a certain danger
in calling such a name – I am no Goody Good that sleeps
in ditches, nor Osburn, drunk and half-witted. She'd dare
not call out such a farmer's wife but there be monstrous
profit in it. She thinks to take my place, John.

PROCTOR   She cannot think it! (*He knows it is true.*)

ELIZABETH   (*reasonably*): John, have you ever shown her somewhat of
contempt? She cannot pass you in the church but you will
blush –

PROCTOR   I may blush for my sin.

ELIZABETH   I think she sees another meaning in that blush.

PROCTOR   And what see you? What see you, Elizabeth?

ELIZABETH   (*conceding*): I think you be somewhat ashamed, for I am
there, and she so close.

PROCTOR   When will you know me, woman? Were I stone I would
have cracked for shame this seven month!

ELIZABETH   Then go and tell her she's a whore. Whatever promise she
may sense – break it, John, break it.

PROCTOR   (*between his teeth*): Good, then. I'll go. (*He starts for his
rifle.*)

ELIZABETH   (*trembling, fearfully*): Oh, how unwillingly!

PROCTOR   (*turning on her, rifle in hand*): I will curse her hotter than
the oldest cinder in hell. But pray, begrudge me not my
anger!

ELIZABETH   Your anger! I only ask you –

PROCTOR   Woman, am I so base? Do you truly think me base?

ELIZABETH   I never called you base.

PROCTOR   Then how do you charge me with such a promise? The
promise that a stallion gives a mare I gave that girl!

ELIZABETH   Then why do you anger with me when I bid you break it?

PROCTOR   Because it speaks deceit, and I am honest! But I'll plead
no more! I see now your spirit twists around the single
error of my life, and I will never tear it free!

ELIZABETH   (*crying out*): You'll tear it free – when you come to know
that I will be your only wife, or no wife at all! She has an

arrow in you yet, John Proctor, and you know it well!

Quite suddenly, as though from the air, a figure appears in the doorway. They start slightly. It is MR HALE. *He is different now – drawn a little, and there is a quality of deference, even of guilt, about his manner now.*

HALE Good evening.

PROCTOR (*still in his shock*): Why, Mr Hale! Good evening to you, sir. Come in, come in.

HALE (*to Elizabeth*): I hope I do not startle you.

ELIZABETH No, no, it's only that I heard no horse –

HALE You are Goodwife Proctor.

PROCTOR Aye; Elizabeth.

HALE (*nods, then*): I hope you're not off to bed yet.

PROCTOR (*setting down his gun*): No, no. (HALE *comes further into the room. And Proctor, to explain his nervousness*): We are not used to visitors after dark, but you're welcome here. Will you sit you down, sir?

HALE I will. (*He sits.*) Let you sit, Goodwife Proctor.

She does, never letting him out of her sight. There is a pause as HALE *looks about the room.*

PROCTOR (*to break the silence*): Will you drink cider, Mr Hale?

HALE No, it rebels my stomach; I have some further travelling yet tonight. Sit you down, sir. (PROCTOR *sits.*) I will not keep you long, but I have some business with you.

PROCTOR Business of the court?

HALE No – no, I come of my own, without the court's authority. Hear me. (*He wets his lips.*) I know not if you are aware, but your wife's name is – mentioned in the court.

PROCTOR We know it, sir. Our Mary Warren told us. We are entirely amazed.

HALE I am a stranger here, as you know. And in my ignorance I find it hard to draw a clear opinion of them that come accused before the court. And so this afternoon, and now tonight, I go from house to house – I come now from Rebecca Nurse's house and –

ELIZABETH	(*shocked*): Rebecca's charged!
HALE	God forbid such a one be charged. She is, however – mentioned somewhat.
ELIZABETH	(*with an attempt at a laugh*): You will never believe, I hope, that Rebecca trafficked with the Devil.
HALE	Woman, it is possible.
PROCTOR	(*taken aback*): Surely, you cannot think so.
HALE	This is a strange time, Mister. No man may longer doubt the powers of the dark are gathered in monstrous attack upon this village. There is too much evidence now to deny it. You will agree, sir?
PROCTOR	(*evading*): I – have no knowledge in that line. But it's hard to think so pious a woman be secretly a Devil's bitch after seventy year of such good prayer.
HALE	Aye. But the Devil is a wily one, you cannot deny it. However, she is far from accused, and I know she will not be. (*Pause.*) I thought, sir, to put some questions as to the Christian character of this house, if you'll permit me.
PROCTOR	(*coldly, resentfully*): Why, we – have no fear of questions sir.
HALE	Good, then. (*He makes himself more comfortable.*) In the book of record that Mr Parris keeps, I note that you are rarely in the church on Sabbath Day.
PROCTOR	No, sir, you are mistaken.
HALE	Twenty-six time in seventeen month, sir. I must call that rare. Will you tell me why you are so absent?
PROCTOR	Mr Hale, I never knew I must account to that man for I come to church or stay home. My wife were sick this winter.
HALE	So I am told. But you, Mister, why could you not come alone?
PROCTOR	I surely did come when I could, and when I could not I prayed in this house.
HALE	Mr Proctor, your house is not a church; your theology must tell you that.

PROCTOR	It does, sir, it does; and it tells me that a minister may pray to God without he have golden candlesticks upon the altar.
HALE	What golden candlesticks?
PROCTOR	Since we built the church there were pewter candlesticks upon the altar; Francis Nurse made them, y'know, and a sweeter hand never touched the metal. But Parris came, and for twenty week he preach nothin' but golden candlesticks until he had them. I labour the earth from dawn of day to blink of night, and I tell you true, when I look to heaven and see my money glaring at his elbows – it hurt my prayer, sir, it hurt my prayer. I think sometimes, the man dreams cathedrals, not clapboard meetin' houses.
HALE	(*thinks, then*): And yet, Mister, a Christian on Sabbath Day must be in church. (*Pause.*) Tell me – you have three children?
PROCTOR	Aye. Boys.
HALE	How comes it that only two are baptized?
PROCTOR	(*starts to speak, then stops, then, as though unable to restrain this*): I like it not that Mr Parris should lay his hand upon my baby. I see no light of God in that man. I'll not conceal it.
HALE	I must say it, Mr Proctor; that is not for you to decide. The man's ordained, therefore the light of God is in him.
PROCTOR	(*flushed with resentment but trying to smile*): What's your suspicion, Mr Hale?
HALE	No, no, I have no –
PROCTOR	I nailed the roof upon the church, I hung the door –
HALE	Oh, did you! That's a good sign, then.
PROCTOR	It may be I have been too quick to bring the man to book, but you cannot think we ever desired the destruction of religion. I think that's in your mind, is it not?
HALE	(*not altogether giving way*): I – have – there is a softness in your record, sir, a softness.
ELIZABETH	I think, maybe, we have been too hard with Mr Parris. I think so. But sure we never loved the Devil here.
HALE	(*nods, deliberating this. Then, with the voice of one administering a secret test*): Do you know your

Commandments, Elizabeth?

ELIZABETH (*without hesitation, even eagerly*): I surely do. There be no mark of blame upon my life, Mr Hale. I am a covenanted Christian woman.

HALE And you, Mister?

PROCTOR (*a trifle unsteady*): I – am sure I do, sir.

HALE (*glances at her open face, then at John, then*): Let you repeat them, if you will.

PROCTOR The Commandments.

HALE Aye.

PROCTOR (*looking off, beginning to sweat*): Thou shalt not kill.

HALE Aye.

PROCTOR (*counting on his fingers*): Thou shalt not steal. Thou shalt not covet they neighbour's goods, nor make unto thee any graven image. Thou shalt not take the name of the Lord in vain; thou shalt have no gods before me. (*With some hesitation.*) Thou shalt remember the Sabbath Day and keep it holy. (*Pause. Then.*) Thou shalt honour thy father and mother. Thou shalt not bear false witness. (*He is stuck. He counts back on his fingers, knowing one is missing.*) Thou shalt not make unto thee any graven image.

HALE You have said that twice, sir.

PROCTOR (*lost*): Aye. (*He is flailing for it.*)

ELIZABETH (*delicately*); Adultery, John.

PROCTOR (*as though a secret arrow had pained his heart*): Aye. (*Trying to grin it away – to Hale.*) You see, sir, between the two of us we do know them all. (HALE *only looks at Proctor, deep in his attempt to define this man.* PROCTOR *grows more uneasy.*) I think it be a small fault.

HALE Theology, sir, is a fortress; no crack in a fortress may be accounted small. (*He rises; he seems worried now. He paces a little, in deep thought.*)

PROCTOR There be no love for Satan in this house, Mister.

HALE I pray it, I pray it dearly. (*He looks to both of them, an attempt at a smile on his face, but his misgivings are clear.*)

Well then – I'll bid you good night.

ELIZABETH (*unable to restrain herself*): Mr Hale. (*He turns.*) I do think you are suspecting me somewhat? Are you not?

HALE (*obviously disturbed – and evasive*): Goody Proctor, I do not judge you. My duty is to add what I may to the godly wisdom of the court. I pray you both good health and good fortune. (*To John.*) Good night, sir. (*He starts out.*)

ELIZABETH (*with a note of desperation*): I think you must tell him, John.

HALE What's that?

ELIZABETH (*restraining a call*): Will you tell him?

Slight pause. HALE *looks questioningly at John.*

PROCTOR (*with difficulty*): I – I have no witness and cannot prove it, except my word be taken. But I know the children's sickness had naught to do with witchcraft.

HALE (*stopped, struck*): Naught to do –?

PROCTOR Mr Parris discovered them sportin' in the woods. They were startled and took sick.

Pause.

HALE Who told you this?

PROCTOR (*hesitates, then*): Abigail Williams.

HALE Abigail!

PROCTOR Aye.

HALE (*his eyes wide*): Abigail Williams told you it had naught to do with witchcraft!

PROCTOR She told me the day you came, sir.

HALE (*suspiciously*): Why – why did you keep this?

PROCTOR I never knew until tonight that the world is gone daft with this nonsense.

HALE Nonsense! Mister, I have myself examined Tituba, Sarah Good, and numerous others that have confessed to dealing with the Devil. They have *confessed* it.

PROCTOR And why not, if they must hang for denyin' it? There are them that will swear to anything before they'll hang; have you never thought of that?

HALE I have. I – I have indeed. (*It is his own suspicion, but he*

resists it. He glances at Elizabeth, then at John.) And you –
would you testify to this in court?

PROCTOR   I – I had not reckoned with goin' into court. But if I must I
           will.

HALE   Do you falter here?

PROCTOR   I falter nothing, but I may wonder if my story will be
           credited in such a court. I do wonder on it, when such a
           steadyminded minister as you will suspicion such a
           woman that never lied, and cannot, and the world knows
           she cannot! I may falter somewhat, Mister; I am no fool.

HALE   (*quietly–it has impressed him*): Proctor, let you open with
           me now, for I have a rumour that troubles me. It's said
           you hold no belief that there may even be witches in the
           world. Is that true, sir?

PROCTOR   – (*he knows this is critical, and is striving against his
           disgust with Hale and with himself for even answering*): I
           know not what I have said, I may have said it. I have
           wondered if there be witches in the world–although I
           cannot believe they come among us now.

HALE   Then you do not believe –

PROCTOR   I have no knowledge of it; the Bible speaks of witches,
           and I will not deny them.

HALE   And you, woman?

ELIZABETH I – I cannot believe it.

HALE   (*shocked*): You cannot!

PROCTOR   Elizabeth, you bewilder him!

ELIZABETH (*to Hale*): I cannot think the Devil may own a woman's
           soul, Mr Hale, when she keeps an upright way, as I have. I
           am a good woman, I know it; and if you believe I may do
           only good work in the world, and yet be secretly bound to
           Satan, then I must tell you, sir, I do not believe it.

HALE   But, woman, you do believe there are witches in –

ELIZABETH If you think that I am one, then I say there are none.

HALE   You surely do not fly against the Gospel, the Gospel –

PROCTOR   She believe in the Gospel, every word!

ELIZABETH   Question Abigail Williams about the Gospel, not myself!

HALE *stares at her.*

PROCTOR   She do not mean to doubt the Gospel, sir, you cannot think it. This be a Christian house, sir, a Christian house.

HALE   God keep you both; let the third child be quickly baptized, and go you without fail each Sunday in to Sabbath prayer; and keep a solemn, quiet way among you. I think –

GILES COREY *appears in doorway.*

GILES   John!

PROCTOR   Giles! What's the matter?

GILES   They take my wife.

FRANCIS NURSE *enters.*

GILES   And his Rebecca!

PROCTOR   (*to Francis*): Rebecca's in the *jail*!

FRANCIS   Aye, Cheever come and take her in his wagon. We've only now come from the jail, and they'll not even let us in to see them.

ELIZABETH   They've surely gone wild now, Mr Hale!

FRANCIS   (*going to Hale*): Reverend Hale! Can you not speak to the Deputy Governor? I'm sure he mistakes these people –

HALE   Pray calm yourself, Mr Nurse.

FRANCIS   My wife is the very brick and mortar of the church, Mr Hale – (*indicating Giles*) – and Martha Corey, there cannot be a woman closer yet to God than Martha.

HALE   How is Rebecca charged, Mr Nurse?

FRANCIS   (*with a mocking, half-hearted laugh*): For murder, she's charged! (*Mockingly quoting the warrant*): 'For the marvellous and supernatural murder of Goody Putnam's babies.' What am I to do, Mr Hale?

HALE   (*turns from Francis, deeply troubled, then*): Believe me, Mr Nurse, if Rebecca Nurse be tainted, then nothing's left to stop the whole green world from burning. Let you rest upon the justice of the court; the court will send her home, I know it.

FRANCIS You cannot mean she will be tried in court!

HALE (*pleading*): Nurse, though our hearts break, we cannot flinch; these are new times, sir. There is a misty plot afoot so subtle we should be criminal to cling to old respects and ancient friendships. I have seen too many frightful proofs in court – the Devil is alive in Salem, and we dare not quail to follow wherever the accusing finger points!

PROCTOR (*angered*): How may such a woman murder children?

HALE (*in great pain*): Man, remember, until an hour before the Devil fell, God thought him beautiful in Heaven.

GILES I never said my wife were a witch, Mr Hale; I only said she were reading books!

HALE Mr Corey, exactly what complaint were made on your wife?

GILES That bloody mongrel Walcott charge her. Y'see, he buy a pig of my wife four or five year ago, and the pig died soon after. So he come dancin' in for his money back. So my Martha, she says to him, 'Walcott, if you haven't the wit to feed a pig properly, you'll not live to own many', she says. Now he goes to court and claims that from that day to this he cannot keep a pig alive for more than four weeks because my Martha bewitch them with her books!

Enter EZEKIEL CHEEVER. *A shocked silence.*

CHEEVER Good evening to you, Proctor.

PROCTOR Why, Mr Cheever. Good evening.

CHEEVER Good evening, all. Good evening, Mr Hale.

PROCTOR I hope you come not on business of the court.

CHEEVER I do, Proctor, aye. I am clerk of the court now, y'know.

Enter MARSHAL HERRICK, *a man in his early thirties, who is somewhat shamefaced at the moment.*

GILES It's a pity, Ezekiel, that an honest tailor might have gone to Heaven must burn in Hell. You'll burn for this, do you know it?

CHEEVER You know yourself I must do as I'm told. You surely know that, Giles. And I'd as lief you'd not be sending me to Hell. I like not the sound of it, I tell you; I like not the sound of it. (*He fears Proctor, but starts to reach inside his coat.*) Now believe me, Proctor, how heavy be the law, all its tonnage I do carry on my back tonight. (*He takes out a warrant.*) I have a warrant for your wife.

PROCTOR (*to Hale*): You said she were not charged!

HALE I know nothin' of it. (*To Cheever.*) When were she charged?

CHEEVER I am given sixteen warrant tonight, sir, and she is one.

PROCTOR Who charged her?

CHEEVER Why, Abigail Williams charge her.

PROCTOR On what proof, what proof?

CHEEVER (*looking about the room*): Mr Proctor, I have little time. The court bid me search your house, but I like not to search a house. So will you hand me any poppets that your wife may keep here?

PROCTOR Poppets?

ELIZABETH I never kept no poppets, not since I were a girl.

CHEEVER (*embarrassed, glancing toward the mantel where sits Mary Warren's poppet*): I spy a poppet, Goody Proctor.

ELIZABETH Oh! (*Going for it.*) Why, this is Mary's.

CHEEVER (*shyly*): Would you please to give it to me?

ELIZABETH (*handing it to him, asks Hale*): Has the court discovered a text in poppets now?

CHEEVER (*carefully holding the poppet*): Do you keep any others in this house?

PROCTOR No, nor this one either till tonight. What signifies a poppet?

CHEEVER Why, a poppet – (*he gingerly turns the poppet over*) – a poppet may signify – Now, woman, will you please to come with me?

PROCTOR She will not! (*To Elizabeth.*) Fetch Mary here.

CHEEVER (*ineptly reaching toward Elizabeth*): No, no, I am forbid to leave her from my sight.

PROCTOR (*pushing his arm away*): You'll leave her out of sight and out of mind, Mister. Fetch Mary, Elizabeth. (ELIZABETH *goes upstairs.*)

HALE What signifies a poppet, Mr Cheever?

CHEEVER (*turning the poppet over in his hands*): Why, they say it may signify that she – (*He has lifted the poppet's skirt, and his eyes widen in astonished fear.*) Why, this, this –

PROCTOR (*reaching for the poppet*): What's there?

CHEEVER Why – (*He draws out a long needle from the poppet.*) – it is a needle! Herrick, Herrick, it is a needle!

HERRICK *comes towards him.*

PROCTOR (*angrily, bewildered*): And what signifies a needle!

CHEEVER (*his hands shaking*): Why, this go hard with her, Proctor, this – I had my doubts, Proctor, I had my doubts, but here's calamity. (*To Hale, showing the needle.*) You see it, sir, it is a needle!

HALE Why? What meanin' has it?

CHEEVER (*wide-eyed, trembling*): The girl, the Williams girl, Abigail Williams, sir. She sat to dinner in Reverend Parris's house tonight, and without word nor warnin' she falls to the floor. Like a struck beast, he says, and screamed a scream that a bull would weep to hear. And he goes to save her, and, stuck two inches in the flesh of her belly, he draw a needle out. And demandin' of her how she come to be so stabbed, she – (*to Proctor now*) – testify it were your wife's familiar spirit pushed it in.

PROCTOR Why, she done it herself! (*To Hale.*) I hope you're not takin' this for proof, Mister!

HALE, *struck by the proof, is silent.*

CHEEVER 'Tis hard proof! (*To Hale.*) I find here a poppet Goody Proctor keeps. I have found it, sir. And in the belly of the poppet a needle's stuck. I tell you true, Proctor, I never warranted to see such proof of Hell, and I bid you obstruct me not, for I –

Enter ELIZABETH *with* MARY. PROCTOR, *seeing Mary Warren, draws her by the arm to Hale.*

PROCTOR Here now! Mary, how did this poppet come into my house?

MARY (*frightened for herself, her voice very small*): What poppet's that, sir?

PROCTOR	(*impatiently, pointing at the doll in Cheever's hand*): This poppet, this poppet.
MARY	(*evasively, looking at it*): Why, I – I think it is mine.
PROCTOR	It is your poppet, is it not?
MARY	(*not understanding the direction of this*): It – is, sir.
PROCTOR	And how did it come into this house?
MARY	(*glancing about at the avid faces*): Why – I made it in the court, sir, and – give to Goody Proctor tonight.
PROCTOR	(*to Hale*): Now, sir – do you have it?
HALE	Mary Warren, a needle have been found inside this poppet.
MARY	(*bewildered*): Why, I meant no harm by it, sir.
PROCTOR	(*quickly*): You stuck that needle in yourself?
MARY	I – I believe I did, sir, I –
PROCTOR	(*to Hale*): What say you now?
HALE	(*watching Mary Warren closely*): Child, you are certain this be your natural memory? May it be, perhaps, that someone conjures you even now to say this?
MARY	Conjures me? Why, no, sir, I am entirely myself, I think. Let you ask Susanna Walcott – she saw me sewin' it in court. (*Or better still.*) Ask Abby, Abby sat beside me when I made it.
PROCTOR	(*to Hale, of Cheever*): Bid him begone. Your mind is surely settled now. Bid him out, Mr Hale.
ELIZABETH	What signifies a needle?
HALE	Mary – you charge a cold and cruel murder on Abigail.
MARY	Murder! I charge no –
HALE	Abigail were stabbed tonight; a needle were found stuck into her belly –
ELIZABETH	And she charges me?
HALE	Aye.
ELIZABETH	(*her breath knocked out*): Why – ! The girl is murder! She must be ripped out of the world!
CHEEVER	(*pointing at Elizabeth*): You've heard that, sir! Ripped out of the world! Herrick, you heard it!

PROCTOR	(*suddenly snatching the warrant out of Cheever's hands*): Out with you.
CHEEVER	Proctor, you dare not touch the warrant.
PROCTOR	(*ripping the warrant*): Out with you!
CHEEVER	You've ripped the Deputy Governor's warrant, man!
PROCTOR	Damn the Deputy Governor! Out of my house!
HALE	Now, Proctor, Proctor!
PROCTOR	Get y'gone with them. You are a broken minister.
HALE	Proctor, if she is innocent, the court –
PROCTOR	If *she* is innocent! Why do you never wonder if Parris be innocent, or Abigail? Is the accuser always holy now? Were they born this morning as clean as God's fingers? I'll tell you what's walking Salem – vengeance is walking Salem. We are what we always were in Salem, but now the little crazy children are jangling the keys of the kingdom, and common vengeance writes the law! This warrant's vengeance! I'll not give my wife to vengeance!
ELIZABETH	I'll go, John –
PROCTOR	You will not go!
HERRICK	I have nine men outside. You cannot keep her. The law binds me, John, I cannot budge.
PROCTOR	(*to Hale, ready to break him*): Will you see her taken?
HALE	Proctor, the court is just–
PROCTOR	Pontius Pilate! God will not let you wash your hands of this!
ELIZABETH	John – I think I must go with them. (*He cannot bear to look at her.*) Mary, there is bread enough for the morning; you will bake, in the afternoon. Help Mr Proctor as you were his daughter – you owe me that, and much more. (*She is fighting her weeping. To Proctor.*) When the children wake, speak nothing of witchcraft – it will frighten them. (*She cannot go on.*)
PROCTOR	I will bring you home. I will bring you soon.
ELIZABETH	Oh, John, bring me soon!

PROCTOR   I will fall like an ocean on that court! Fear nothing,
Elizabeth.

ELIZABETH   (*with great fear*): I will fear nothing. (*She looks about the
room, as though to fix it in her mind.*) Tell the children I
have gone to visit someone sick.

She walks out the door, HERRICK *and* CHEEVER *behind her.
For a moment,* PROCTOR *watches from the doorway. The
clank of chain is heard.*

PROCTOR   Herrick! Herrick, don't chain her! (*He rushes out the door.
From outside.*) Damn you, man, you will not chain her! Off
with them! I'll not have it! I will not have her chained!

There are other men's voices against his. HALE, *in a fever of
guilt and uncertainty, turns from the door to avoid the
sight;* MARY WARREN *bursts into tears and sits weeping.* GILES
calls to Hale.

GILES   And yet silent, minister? It is fraud, you know it is fraud!
What keeps you, man?

PROCTOR *is half braced, half pushed into the room by two
deputies and Herrick.*

PROCTOR   I'll pay you, Herrick, I will surely pay you!

HERRICK   (*panting*): In God's name, John, I cannot help myself. I
must chain them all. Now let you keep inside this house
till I am gone! (*He goes out with his deputies.*)

PROCTOR *stands there, gulping air. Horses and a wagon
creaking are heard.*

HALE   (*in great uncertainty*): Mr Proctor –

PROCTOR   Out of my sight!

HALE   Charity, Proctor, charity. What I have heard in her favour, I
will not fear to testify in court. God help me, I cannot
judge her guilty or innocent – I know not. Only this
consider: the world goes mad, and it profit nothing you
should lay the cause to the vengeance of a little girl.

PROCTOR   You are a coward! Though you be ordained in God's own
tears, you are a coward now!

HALE   Proctor, I cannot think God be provoked so grandly by such a petty cause. The jails are packed – our greatest judges sit in Salem now – and hangin's promised. Man, we must look to cause proportionate. Were there murder done, perhaps, and never brought to light? Abomination? Some secret blasphemy that stinks to Heaven? Think on cause, man, and let you help me to discover it. For there's your way, believe it, there is your only way, when such confusion strikes upon the world. (*He goes to Giles and Francis.*) Let you counsel among yourselves; think on your village and what may have drawn from heaven such thundering wrath upon you all. I shall pray God open up our eyes.

HALE *goes out.*

FRANCIS (*struck by Hale's mood*): I never heard no murder done in Salem.

PROCTOR – (*he has been reached by Hale's words*): Leave me, Francis, leave me.

GILES (*shaken*): John –tell me, are we lost?

PROCTOR Go home now, Giles. We'll speak on it tomorrow.

GILES Let you think on it. We'll come early, eh?

PROCTOR Aye. Go now, Giles.

GILES Good night, then.

GILES COREY *goes out. After a moment:*

MARY (*in a fearful squeak of a voice*): Mr Proctor, very likely they'll let her come home once they're given proper evidence.

PROCTOR You're coming to the court with me, Mary. You will tell it in court.

MARY I cannot charge murder on Abigail.

PROCTOR (*moving menacingly toward her*): You will tell the court how that poppet come here and who stuck the needle in.

MARY She'll kill me for sayin' that! (*Proctor continues toward her.*) Abby'll charge lechery on you, Mr Proctor!

PROCTOR (*halting*): She's told you!

MARY I have known it, sir. She'll ruin you with it, I know she will.

PROCTOR (*hesitating, and with deep hatred of himself*): Good. Then her saintliness is done with. (MARY *back from him.*) We will slide together into our pit; you will tell the court what you know.

MARY (*in terror*): I cannot, they'll turn on me –

PROCTOR *strides and catches her, and she is repeating, 'I cannot, I cannot!'*

PROCTOR My wife will never die for me! I will bring your guts into your mouth but that goodness will not die for me!

MARY (*struggling to escape him*): I cannot do it, I cannot!

PROCTOR (*grasping her by the throat as though he would strangle her*): Make your peace with it! Now Hell and Heaven grapple on our backs, and all our old pretence is ripped away – make your peace! (*He throws her to the floor, where she sobs, 'I cannot, I cannot . . .' And now, half to himself, staring, and turning to the open door.*): Peace. It is a providence, and no great change; we are only what we always were, but naked now. (*He walks as though toward a great horror, facing the open sky.*) Aye, naked! And the wind, God's icy wind, will blow!

And she is over and over again sobbing, 'I cannot, I cannot, I cannot', as

THE CURTAIN FALLS

ACT THREE

The vestry room of the Salem meeting house, now serving as the anteroom of the General Court.

As the curtain rises, the room is empty, but for sunlight pouring through two high windows in the back wall. The room is solemn, even forbidding. Heavy beams jut out, boards of random widths make up the walls. At the right are two doors leading into the meeting house proper, where the court is being held. At the left another door leads outside.

There is a plain bench at the left, and another at the right. In the centre a rather long meeting table, with stools and a considerable armchair snugged up to it.

Through the partitioning wall at the right we hear a prosecutor's voice, JUDGE HATHORNE'*s, asking a question; then a woman's voice,* MARTHA COREY'*s, replying.*

HATHORNE'S VOICE	Now, Martha Corey, there is abundant evidence in our hands to show that you have given yourself to the reading of fortunes. Do you deny it?
MARTHA COREY'S VOICE	I am innocent to a witch. I know not what a witch is.
HATHORNE'S VOICE	How do you know, then, that you are not a witch?
MARTHA COREY'S VOICE	If I were, I would know it.
HATHORNE'S VOICE	Why do you hurt these children?
MARTHA COREY'S VOICE	I do not hurt them. I scorn it!
GILES' VOICE	(*roaring*): I have evidence for the court!
	Voices of townspeople rise in excitement.
DANFORTH'S VOICE	You will keep your seat!
GILES' VOICE	Thomas Putnam is reaching out for land!
DANFORTH'S VOICE	Remove that man, Marshal!

GILES' VOICE You're hearing lies, lies!

A roaring goes up from the people.

HATHORNE'S VOICE Arrest him, excellency!

GILES' VOICE I have evidence. Why will you not hear my evidence?

The door opens and Giles is half carried into the vestry room by HERRICK.

GILES Hands off, damn you, let me go!

HERRICK Giles, Giles!

GILES Out of my way, Herrick, I bring evidence –

HERRICK You cannot go in there, Giles; it's a court!

Enter HALE *from the court.*

HALE Pray be calm a moment.

GILES You, Mr Hale, go in there and demand I speak.

HALE A moment, sir, a moment.

GILES They'll be hangin' my wife!

JUDGE HATHORNE enters. He is in his sixties, a bitter, remorseless Salem judge.

HATHORNE How do you dare come roarin' into this court! Are you gone daft, Corey!

GILES You're not a Boston judge yet, Hathorne. You'll not call me daft!

Enter DEPUTY-GOVERNOR DANFORTH *and, behind him,* EZEKIEL CHEEVER *and* PARRIS. *On his appearance, silence falls.* DANFORTH *is a grave man in his sixties, of some humour and sophistication that does not, however, interfere with an exact loyalty to his position and his cause. He comes down to* GILES, *who awaits his wrath.*

DANFORTH (*looking directly at Giles*): Who is this man?

PARRIS Giles Corey, sir, and a more contentious –

GILES (*to Parris*): I am asked the question, and I am old enough to answer it! (*To Danforth, who impresses him and to whom he smiles through his strain.*) My name is Corey, sir, Giles Corey. I have six hundred acres, and timber in addition. It is my wife you be condemning now. (*He indicates the courtroom.*)

DANFORTH	And how do you imagine to help her cause with such contemptuous riot? Now be gone. Your old age alone keeps you out of jail for this.
GILES	(*beginning to plead*): They be tellin' lies about my wife, sir, I –
DANFORTH	Do you take it upon yourself to determine what this court shall believe and what it shall set aside?
GILES	Your Excellency, we mean no disrespect for –
DANFORTH	Disrespect indeed! It is disruption, Mister. This is the highest court of the supreme government of this province, do you know it?
GILES	(*beginning to weep*): Your Excellency, I only said she were readin' books, sir, and they come and take her out of my house for –
DANFORTH	(*mystified*): Books! What books?
GILES	(*through helpless sobs*): It is my third wife, sir; I never had no wife that be so taken with books, and I thought to find the cause of it, d'y'see, but it were no witch I blamed her for. (*He is openly weeping.*) I have broke charity with the woman, I have broke charity with her. (*He covers his face, ashamed.* DANFORTH *is respectfully silent.*)
HALE	Excellency, he claims hard evidence for his wife's defence. I think that in all justice you must –
DANFORTH	Then let him submit his evidence in proper affidavit. You are certainly aware of our procedure here, Mr Hale. (*To Herrick.*) Clear this room.
HERRICK	Come now, Giles. (*He pushes Corey out.*)
FRANCIS	We are desperate, sir; we come here three days now and cannot be heard.
DANFORTH	Who is this man?
FRANCIS	Francis Nurse, Your Excellency.
HALE	His wife's Rebecca that were condemned this morning.
DANFORTH	Indeed! I am amazed to find you in such uproar. I have only good report of your character, Mr Nurse.
HATHORNE	I think they must both be arrested in contempt, sir.

DANFORTH	(*to Francis*): Let you write your plea, and in due time I will –
FRANCIS	Excellency, we have proof for your eyes; God forbid you shut them to it. The girls, sir, the girls are frauds.
DANFORTH	What's that?
FRANCIS	We have proof of it, sir. They are all deceiving you.
	DANFORTH is *shocked, but studying Francis.*
HATHORNE	This is contempt, sir, contempt!
DANFORTH	Peace, Judge Hathorne. Do you know who I am, Mr Nurse?
FRANCIS	I surely do, sir, and I think you must be a wise judge to be what you are.
DANFORTH	And do you know that near to four hundred are in the jails from Marblehead to Lynn, and upon my signature?
FRANCIS	I –
DANFORTH	And seventy-two condemned to hang by that signature?
FRANCIS	Excellency, I never thought to say it to such a weighty judge, but you are deceived.
	Enter GILES *from left. All turn to see as he beckons in Mary Warren with Proctor.* MARY *is keeping her eyes to the ground;* PROCTOR *has her elbow as though she were near collapse.*
PARRIS	(*on seeing her, in shock*): Mary Warren! (*He goes directly to bend close to her face.*) What are you about here?
PROCTOR	(*pressing Parris away from her with a gentle but firm motion of protectiveness*): She would speak with the Deputy Governor.
DANFORTH	(*shocked by this, turns to Herrick*): Did you not tell me Mary Warren were sick in bed?
HERRICK	She were, Your Honour. When I go to fetch her to the court last week, she said she were sick.
GILES	She has been strivin' with her soul all week, Your Honour; she comes now to tell the truth of this to you.
DANFORTH	Who is this?
PROCTOR	John Proctor, sir. Elizabeth Proctor is my wife.

PARRIS	Beware this man, Your Excellency, this man is mischief.
HALE	(*excitedly*): I think you must hear the girl, sir, she –
DANFORTH	(*who has become very interested in Mary Warren and only raises a hand toward Hale*): Peace. What would you tell us, Mary Warren?
	PROCTOR *looks at her, but she cannot speak.*
PROCTOR	She never saw no spirits, sir.
DANFORTH	(*with great alarm and surprise, to Mary*): Never saw no spirits!
GILES	(*eagerly*): Never.
PROCTOR	(*reaching into his jacket*): She has signed a deposition, sir –
DANFORTH	(*instantly*): No, no, I accept no depositions. (*He is rapidly calculating this; he turns from her to Proctor.*) Tell me, Mr Proctor, have you given out this story in the village?
PROCTOR	We have not.
PARRIS	They've come to overthrow the court, sir! This man is –
DANFORTH	I pray you, Mr Parris. Do you know, Mr Proctor, that the entire contention of the state in these trials is that the voice of Heaven is speaking through the children?
PROCTOR	I know that, sir.
DANFORTH	(*thinks, staring at Proctor, then turns to Mary Warren*): And you, Mary Warren, how came you to cry out people for sending their spirits against you?
MARY	It were pretence, sir.
DANFORTH	I cannot hear you.
PROCTOR	It were pretence, she says.
DANFORTH	Ah? And the other girls? Susanna Walcott, and the others? They are also pretending?
MARY	Aye, sir.
DANFORTH	(*wide-eyed*): Indeed. (*Pause. He is baffled by this. He turns to study Proctor's face.*)
PARRIS	(*in a sweat*): Excellency, you surely cannot think to let so vile a lie be spread in open court!
DANFORTH	Indeed not, but it strike hard upon me that she will dare to come here with such a tale. Now, Mr Proctor, before I

	decide whether I shall hear you or not, it is my duty to tell you this. We burn a hot fire here; it melts down all concealment.
PROCTOR	I know that, sir.
DANFORTH	Let me continue. I understand well, a husband's tenderness may drive him to extravagance in defence of a wife. Are you certain in your conscience, Mister, that your evidence is the truth?
PROCTOR	It is. And you will surely know it.
DANFORTH	And you thought to declare this revelation in the open court before the public?
PROCTOR	I thought I would, aye – with your permission.
DANFORTH	(*his eyes narrowing*): Now, sir, what is your purpose in so doing?
PROCTOR	Why, I – I would free my wife, sir.
DANFORTH	There lurks nowhere in your heart, nor hidden in your spirit, any desire to undermine this court?
PROCTOR	(*with the faintest faltering*): Why, no, sir.
CHEEVER	(*clears his throat, awakening*): I – Your Excellency.
DANFORTH	Mr Cheever.
CHEEVER	I think it be my duty, sir – (*kindly, to Proctor*). You'll not deny it, John. (*To Danforth.*) When we come to take his wife, he damned the court and ripped your warrant.
PARRIS	Now you have it!
DANFORTH	He did that, Mr Hale?
HALE	(*takes a breath*): Aye, he did.
PROCTOR	It were a temper, sir. I knew not what I did.
DANFORTH	(*studying him*): Mr Proctor.
PROCTOR	Aye, sir.
DANFORTH	(*straight into his eyes*): Have you ever seen the Devil?
PROCTOR	No sir.
DANFORTH	You are in all respects a Gospel Christian?
PROCTOR	I am, sir.
PARRIS	Such a Christian that will not come to church but once in a month!
DANFORTH	(*restrained – he is curious*): Not come to church?

PROCTOR	I – I have no love for Mr Parris. It is no secret. But God I surely love.
CHEEVER	He plough on Sunday, sir.
DANFORTH	Plough on Sunday!
CHEEVER	(*apologetically*): I think it be evidence, John. I am an official of the court, I cannot keep it.
PROCTOR	I – I have once or twice ploughed on Sunday. I have three children, sir, and until last year my land give little.
GILES	You'll find other Christians that do plough on Sunday if the truth be known.
HALE	Your Honour, I cannot think you may judge the man on such evidence.
DANFORTH	I judge nothing. (*Pause. He keeps watching Proctor, who tries to meet his gaze.*) I tell you straight, Mister – I have seen marvels in this court. I have seen people choked before my eyes by spirits; I have seen them struck by pins and slashed by daggers. I have until this moment not the slightest reason to suspect that the children may be deceiving me. Do you understand my meaning?
PROCTOR	Excellency, does it not strike upon you that so many of these women have lived so long with such upright reputation, and –
PARRIS	Do you read the Gospel, Mr Proctor?
PROCTOR	I read the Gospel.
PARRIS	I think not, or you should surely know that Cain were an upright man, and yet he did kill Abel.
PROCTOR	Aye, God tells us that. (*To Danforth.*) But who tells us Rebecca Nurse murdered seven babies by sending out her spirit on them? It is the children only, and this one will swear she lied to you.

DANFORTH *considers, then beckons Hathorne to him.*

HATHORNE *leans in, and he speaks in his ear.* HATHORNE *nods.*

HATHORNE	Aye, she's the one.
DANFORTH	Mr Proctor, this morning, your wife send me a claim in which she states that she is pregnant now.

PROCTOR	My wife pregnant!
DANFORTH	There be no sign of it – we have examined her body.
PROCTOR	But if she say she is pregnant then she must be! That woman will never lie, Mr Danforth.
DANFORTH	She will not?
PROCTOR	Never, sir, never.
DANFORTH	We have thought it too convenient to be credited. However, if I should tell you now that I will let her be kept another month; and if she begin to show her natural signs, you shall have her living yet another year until she is delivered–what say you to that? (JOHN PROCTOR *is struck silent.*) Come now. You say your only purpose is to save your wife. Good, then, she is saved at least this year, and a year is long. What say you, sir? It is done now. (*In conflict,* PROCTOR *glances at Francis and Giles.*) Will you drop this charge?
PROCTOR	I – I think I cannot.
DANFORTH	(*now an almost imperceptible hardness in his voice*): Then your purpose is somewhat larger.
PARRIS	He's come to overthrow this court, Your Honour!
PROCTOR	These are my friends. Their wives are also accused –
DANFORTH	(*with a sudden briskness of manner*): I judge you not, sir. I am ready to hear your evidence.
PROCTOR	I come not to hurt the court; I only –
DANFORTH	(*cutting him off*): Marshal, go into the court and bid Judge Stoughton and Judge Sewall declare recess for one hour. And let them go to the tavern, if they will. All witnesses and prisoners are to be kept in the building.
HERRICK	Aye, sir. (*Very deferentially.*) If I may say it, sir, I know this man all my life. It is a good man, sir.
DANFORTH	– (*it is the reflection on himself he resents*): I am sure of it, Marshal. (HERRICK *nods, then goes out.*) Now, what deposition do you have for us, Mr Proctor? And I beg you be clear, open as the sky, and honest.
PROCTOR	(*as he takes out several papers*): I am no lawyer, so I'll –

DANFORTH   The pure in heart need no lawyers. Proceed as you will.

PROCTOR   (*handing Danforth a paper*): Will you read this first, sir?
It's a sort of testament. The people signing it declare their
good opinion of Rebecca, and my wife, and Martha Corey.
(DANFORTH *looks down at the paper.*)

PARRIS   (*to enlist Danforth's sarcasm*): Their good opinion! (*But*
DANFORTH *goes on reading, and* PROCTOR *is heartened.*)

PROCTOR   These are all landholding farmers, members of the church.
(*Delicately, trying to point out a paragraph.*) If you'll
notice, sir – they've known the women many years and
never saw no sign they had dealing with the Devil.

PARRIS *nervously moves over and reads over Danforth's
shoulder.*

DANFORTH   (*glancing down a long list*): How many names are here?

FRANCIS   Ninety-one, Your Excellency.

PARRIS   (*sweating*): These people should be summoned. (DANFORTH
looks up at him questioningly.) For questioning.

FRANCIS   (*trembling with anger*): Mr Danforth, I gave them all my
word no harm would come to them for signing this.

PARRIS   This is a clear attack upon the court!

HALE   (*to Parris, trying to contain himself*): Is every defence an
attack upon the court? Can no one – ?

PARRIS   All innocent and Christian people are happy for the courts
in Salem! These people are gloomy for it. (*To Danforth
directly.*) And I think you will want to know, from each
and every one of them, what discontents them with you!

HATHORNE   I think they ought to be examined, sir.

DANFORTH   It is not necessarily an attack, I think. Yet –

FRANCIS   These are all covenanted Christians, sir.

DANFORTH   Then I am sure they may have nothing to fear. (*Hands
Cheever the paper.*) Mr Cheever, have warrants drawn for
all of these – arrest for examination. (*To Proctor.*) Now,
Mister, what other information do you have for us? (FRANCIS
is still standing, horrified.) You may sit, Mr Nurse.

FRANCIS   I have brought trouble on these people; I have –

DANFORTH   No, old man, you have not hurt these people if they are of good conscience. But you must understand, sir, that a person is either with this court or he must be counted against it, there be no road between. This is a sharp time, now, a precise time – we live no longer in the dusky afternoon when evil mixed itself with good and befuddled the world. Now, by God's grace, the shining sun is up, and them that fear not light will surely praise it. I hope you will be one of those. (MARY WARREN *suddenly sobs.*) She's not hearty, I see.

PROCTOR   No, she's not, sir. (*To* MARY, *bending to her, holding her hand, quietly.*) Now, remember what the angel Raphael said to the boy Tobias. Remember it.

MARY   (*hardly audible*): Aye.

PROCTOR   'Do that which is good, and no harm shall come to thee.'

MARY   Aye.

DANFORTH   Come, man, we wait you.

     MARSHAL HERRICK *returns, and takes his post at the door.*

GILES   John, my deposition, give him mine.

PROCTOR   Aye. (*He hands Danforth another paper.*) This is Mr Corey's deposition.

DANFORTH   Oh? (*He looks down at it. Now* HATHORNE *comes behind him and reads with him.*)

HATHORNE   (*suspiciously*): What lawyer drew this, Corey?

GILES   You know I never hired a lawyer in my life, Hathorne.

DANFORTH   (*finishing the reading*): It is very well phrased. My compliments. Mr Parris, if Mr Putnam is in the court, will you bring him in? (HATHORNE *takes the deposition, and walks to the window with it.* PARRIS *goes into the court.*) You have no legal training, Mr Corey?

GILES   (*very pleased*): I have the best, sir – I am thirty-three time in court in my life. And always plaintiff, too.

DANFORTH   Oh, then you're much put-upon.

GILES   I am never put-upon; I know my rights, sir. And I will

have them. You know, your father tried a case of mine –
might be thirty-five year ago, I think.

DANFORTH Indeed.

GILES He never spoke to you of it?

DANFORTH No, I cannot recall it.

GILES That's strange, he give me nine pounds damages. He were
a fair judge, your father. Y'see, I had a white mare that
time, and this fellow come to borrow the mare – (*Enter*
PARRIS *with* THOMAS PUTNAM. *When he sees Putnam, Giles'
ease goes; he is hard.*) Aye, there he is.

DANFORTH Mr Putnam. I have here an accusation by Mr Corey against
you. He states that you coldly prompted your daughter to
cry witchery upon George Jacobs that is now in jail.

PUTNAM It is a lie.

DANFORTH (*turning to Giles*): Mr Putnam states your charge is a lie.
What say you to that?

GILES (*furious, his fists clenched*): A fart on Thomas Putnam, that
is what I say to that!

DANFORTH What proof do you submit for your charge, sir?

GILES My proof is there! (*Pointing to the paper.*) If Jacobs hangs
for a witch he forfeit up his property – that's law! And
there is none but Putnam with the coin to buy so great a
piece. This man is killing his neighbours for that land!

DANFORTH But proof, sir, proof.

GILES (*pointing to his deposition*): The proof is there! I have it
from an honest man who heard Putnam say it! The day his
daughter cried out on Jacobs, he said she'd given him a
fair gift of land.

HATHORNE And the name of this man?

GILES (*taken aback*): What name?

HATHORNE The man that give you this information.

GILES (*hesitates, then*): Why, I – I cannot give you his name.

HATHORNE And why not?

GILES (*hesitates, then bursts out*): You know well why not! He'll
lay in jail if I give his name!

HATHORNE	This is contempt of the court, Mr Danforth!
DANFORTH	(*to avoid that*): You will surely tell us the name.
GILES	I will not give you no name. I mentioned my wife's name once and I'll burn in hell long enough for that. I stand mute.
DANFORTH	In that case, I have no choice but to arrest you for contempt of this court, do you know that?
GILES	This is a hearing; you cannot clap me for contempt of a hearing.
DANFORTH	Oh, it is a proper lawyer! Do you wish me to declare the court in full session here? Or will you give me good reply?
GILES	(*faltering*): I cannot give you no name, sir, I cannot.
DANFORTH	You are a foolish old man. Mr Cheever, begin the record. The court is now in session. I ask you, Mr Corey –
PROCTOR	(*breaking in*): Your Honour – he has the story in confidence, sir, and he –
PARRIS	The Devil lives on such confidences! (*To Danforth.*) Without confidences there could be no conspiracy, Your Honour!
HATHORNE	I think it must be broken, sir.
DANFORTH	(*to Giles*): Old man, if your informant tells the truth let him come here openly like a decent man. But if he hide in anonymity I must know why. Now sir, the government and central church demand of you the name of him who reported Mr Thomas Putnam a common murderer.
HALE	Excellency –
DANFORTH	Mr Hale.
HALE	We cannot blink it more. There is a prodigious fear of this court in the country –
DANFORTH	Then there is a prodigious guilt in the country. Are you afraid to be questioned here?
HALE	I may only fear the Lord, sir, but there is fear in the country nevertheless.
DANFORTH	(*angered now*): Reproach me not with the fear in the country, there is fear in the country because there is a moving plot to topple Christ in the country!

HALE   But it does not follow that everyone accused is part of it.

DANFORTH No uncorrupted man may fear this court, Mr Hale! None!
              (*To Giles.*) You are under arrest in contempt of this court.
              Now sit you down and take counsel with yourself, or you
              will be set in the jail until you decide to answer all
              questions.

              GILES COREY *makes a rush for Putnam.* PROCTOR *lunges and*
              holds him.

PROCTOR   No, Giles!

GILES   (*over Proctor's shoulder at Putnam*): I'll cut your throat,
              Putnam, I'll kill you yet!

PROCTOR   (*forcing him into a chair*): Peace, Giles, peace. (*Releasing*
              him.) We'll prove ourselves. Now we will. (*He starts to*
              turn to Danforth.)

GILES   Say nothin' more, John. (*Pointing at Danforth.*) He's only
              playin' you! He means to hang us all!

              MARY *bursts into sobs.*

DANFORTH This is a court of law, Mister. I'll have no effrontery
              here!

PROCTOR   Forgive him, sir, for his old age. Peace, Giles, we'll prove
              it all now. (*He lifts up Mary's chin.*) You cannot weep,
              Mary. Remember the angel, what he say to the boy. Hold
              to it, now; there is your rock. (MARY *quiets. He takes out a*
              paper, and turns to Danforth.) This is Mary Warren's
              deposition. I – I would ask you remember, sir, while you
              read it, that until two weeks ago she were no different
              than the other children are today. (*He is speaking*
              reasonably, restraining all his fears, his anger, his anxiety.)
              You saw her scream, she howled, she swore familiar
              spirits choked her; she even testified that Satan, in the
              form of women now in jail, tried to win her soul away,
              and then when she refused –

DANFORTH We know all this.

PROCTOR   Aye, sir. She swears now that she never saw Satan; nor
              any spirit, vague or clear, that Satan may have sent to hurt
              her. And she declares her friends are lying now.

PROCTOR *starts to hand Danforth the deposition, and* HALE *comes up to Danforth in a trembling state.*

HALE   Excellency, a moment. I think this goes to the heart of the matter.

DANFORTH (*with deep misgivings*): It surely does.

HALE   I cannot say he is an honest man; I know him little. But in all justice, sir, a claim so weighty cannot be argued by a farmer. In God's name, sir, stop here; send him home and let him come again with a lawyer –

DANFORTH (*patiently*): Now look you, Mr Hale –

HALE   Excellency, I have signed seventy-two death warrants; I am a minister of the Lord, and I dare not take a life without there be a proof so immaculate no slightest qualm of conscience may doubt it.

DANFORTH Mr Hale, you surely do not doubt my justice.

HALE   I have this morning signed away the soul of Rebecca Nurse, Your Honour. I'll not conceal it, my hand shakes yet as with a wound! I pray you, sir, *this* argument let lawyers present to you.

DANFORTH Mr Hale, believe me; for a man of such terrible learning you are most bewildered – I hope you will forgive me. I have been thirty-two year at the bar, sir, and I should be confounded were I called upon to defend these people. Let you consider, now – (*To Proctor and the others.*) And I bid you all do likewise. In an ordinary crime, how does one defend the accused? One calls up witnesses to prove his innocence. But witchcraft is *ipso facto,* on its face and by its nature, an invisible crime, is it not? Therefore, who may possibly be witness to it? The witch and the victim. None other. Now we cannot hope the witch will accuse herself; granted? Therefore, we must rely upon her victims – and they do testify, the children certainly do testify. As for the witches, none will deny that we are most eager for all their confessions. Therefore, what is left for a lawyer to bring out? I think I have made my point. Have I not?

HALE   But this child claims the girls are not truthful, and if they are not –

DANFORTH That is precisely what I am about to consider, sir. What more may you ask of me? Unless you doubt my probity?

HALE   (*defeated*): I surely do not, sir. Let you consider it, then.

DANFORTH And let you put your heart to rest. Her deposition, Mr Proctor.

PROCTOR *hands it to him.* HATHORNE *rises, goes beside Danforth, and starts reading.* PARRIS *comes to his other side.* DANFORTH *looks at John Proctor, then proceeds to read.* HALE *gets up, finds position near the judge, reads too.* PROCTOR *glances at Giles.* FRANCIS *prays silently, hands pressed together.* CHEEVER *waits placidly, the sublime official, dutiful.* MARY WARREN *sobs once.* PROCTOR *touches her head reassuringly. Presently* DANFORTH *lifts his eyes, stands up, takes out a kerchief and blows his nose. The others stand aside as he moves in thought toward the window.*

PARRIS   (*hardly able to contain his anger and fear*): I should like to question –

DANFORTH – (*his first real outburst, in which his contempt for Parris is clear*): Mr Parris, I bid you be silent! (*He stands in silence, looking out the window. Now, having established that he will set the gait.*) Mr Cheever, will you go into the court and bring the children here? (CHEEVER *gets up and goes out upstage.* DANFORTH *now turns to Mary.*) Mary Warren, how came you to this turnabout? Has Mr Proctor threatened you for this deposition?

MARY   No, sir.

DANFORTH Has he ever threatened you?

MARY   (*weaker*): No, sir.

DANFORTH (*sensing a weakening*): Has he threatened you?

MARY   No, sir.

DANFORTH Then you tell me that you sat in my court, callously lying, when you knew that people would hang by your evidence? (*She does not answer.*) Answer me!

MARY (*almost inaudibly*): I did, sir.

DANFORTH How were you instructed in your life? Do you not know that God damns all liars? (*She cannot speak.*) Or is it now that you lie?

MARY No, sir – I am with God now.

DANFORTH You are with God now.

MARY Aye, sir.

DANFORTH (*containing himself*): I will tell you this – you are either lying now, or you were lying in the court, and in either case you have committed perjury and you will go to jail for it. You cannot lightly say you lied, Mary. Do you know that?

MARY I cannot lie no more. I am with God, I am with God.

But she breaks into sobs at the thought of it, and the right door opens, and enter SUSANNA WALCOTT, MERCY LEWIS, BETTY PARRIS, *and finally* ABIGAIL. CHEEVER *comes to Danforth.*

CHEEVER Ruth Putnam's not in the court, sir, nor the other children.

DANFORTH These will be sufficient. Sit you down, children. (*Silently they sit.*) Your friend, Mary Warren, has given us a deposition. In which she swears that she never saw familiar spirits, apparitions nor any manifest of the Devil. She claims as well that none of you have seen these things either. (*Slight pause.*) Now, children, this is a court of law. The law, based upon the Bible, and the Bible, writ by Almighty God, forbid the practice of witchcraft, and describe death as the penalty thereof. But likewise, children, the law and Bible damn all bearers of false witness. (*Slight pause.*) Now then. It does not escape me that this deposition may be devised to blind us; it may well be that Mary Warren has been conquered by Satan, who sends her here to distract our sacred purpose. If so, her neck will break for it. But if she speak true, I bid you drop now your guile and confess your pretence, for a quick confession will go easier with you. (*Pause.*) Abigail Williams, rise. (ABIGAIL *slowly rises.*) Is there any truth in this?

ABIGAIL	No, sir.
DANFORTH	(*thinks, glances at Mary, then back to Abigail*): Children, a very augur bit will now be turned into your souls until your honesty is proved. Will either of you change your positions now, or do you force me to hard questioning?
ABIGAIL	I have naught to change, sir. She lies.
DANFORTH	(*to Mary*): You would still go on with this?
MARY	(*faintly*): Aye, sir.
DANFORTH	(*turning to Abigail*): A poppet were discovered in Mr Proctor's house, stabbed by a needle. Mary Warren claims that you sat beside her in the court when she made it, and that you saw her make it and witnessed how she herself stuck her needle into it for safe-keeping. What say you to that?
ABIGAIL	(*with a slight note of indignation*): It is a lie, sir.
DANFORTH	(*after a slight pause.*) While you worked for Mr Proctor, did you see poppets in that house?
ABIGAIL	Goody Proctor always kept poppets.
PROCTOR	Your Honour, my wife never kept no poppets. Mary Warren confesses it was her poppet.
CHEEVER	Your Excellency.
DANFORTH	Mr Cheever.
CHEEVER	When I spoke with Goody Proctor in that house, she said she never kept no poppets. But she said she did keep poppets when she were a girl.
PROCTOR	She has not been a girl these fifteen years, Your Honour.
HATHORNE	But a poppet will keep fifteen years, will it not?
PROCTOR	It will keep if it is kept, but Mary Warren swears she never saw no poppets in my house, nor anyone else.
PARRIS	Why could there not have been poppets hid where no one ever saw them?
PROCTOR	(*furious*): There might also be a dragon with five legs in my house, but no one has ever seen it.
PARRIS	We are here, Your Honour, precisely to discover what no one has ever seen.
PROCTOR	Mr Danforth, what profit this girl to turn herself

about? What may Mary Warren gain but hard questioning and worse?

DANFORTH   You are charging Abigail Williams with a marvellous cool plot to murder, do you understand that?

PROCTOR   I do, sir. I believe she means to murder.

DANFORTH   (*pointing at Abigail, incredulously*): This child would murder your wife?

PROCTOR   It is not a child. Now hear me, sir. In the sight of the congregation she were twice this year put out of this meetin' house for laughter during prayer.

DANFORTH   (*shocked, turning to Abigail*): What's this? Laughter during – !

PARRIS   Excellency, she were under Tituba's power at that time, but she is solemn now.

GILES   Aye, now she is solemn and goes to hang people!

DANFORTH   Quiet, man.

HATHORNE   Surely it have no bearing on the question, sir. He charges contemplation of murder.

DANFORTH   Aye. (*He studies Abigail for a moment, then*) Continue, Mr Proctor.

PROCTOR   Mary, now tell the Governor how you danced in the woods.

PARRIS   (*instantly*): Excellency, since I come to Salem this man is blackening my name. He –

DANFORTH   In a moment, sir. (*To Mary Warren, sternly, and surprised.*) What is this dancing?

MARY   I – (*she glances at Abigail, who is staring down at her remorselessly. Then, appealing to Proctor*) Mr Proctor –

PROCTOR   (*taking it right up*): Abigail leads the girls to the woods, Your Honour, and they have danced there naked –

PARRIS   Your Honour, this –

PROCTOR   (*at once*): Mr Parris discovered them himself in the dead of night! There's the 'child' she is!

DANFORTH   (*it is growing into a nightmare, and he turns, astonished, to Parris*): Mr Parris –

PARRIS	I can only say, sir, that I never found any of them naked and this man is –
DANFORTH	But you discovered them dancing in the woods? (*Eyes on Parris, he points at Abigail.*) Abigail?
HALE	Excellency, when I first arrived from Beverly, Mr Parris told me that.
DANFORTH	Do you deny it, Mr Parris?
PARRIS	I do not, sir, but I never saw any of them naked.
DANFORTH	But she have danced?
PARRIS	(*unwillingly*): Aye, sir.
	DANFORTH, *as though with new eyes, looks at Abigail.*
HATHORNE	Excellency, will you permit me? (*He points at Mary Warren.*)
DANFORTH	(*with great worry*): Pray, proceed.
HATHORNE	You say you never saw no spirits, Mary, were never threatened or afflicted by any manifest of the Devil or the Devil's agents.
MARY	(*very faintly*): No, sir.
HATHORNE	(*with a gleam of victory*): And yet, when people accused of witchery confronted you in court, you would faint, saying their spirits came out of their bodies and choked you –
MARY	That were pretence, sir.
DANFORTH	I cannot hear you.
MARY	Pretence, sir.
PARRIS	But you did turn cold, did you not? I myself picked you up many times, and your skin were icy. Mr Danforth, you –
DANFORTH	I saw that many times.
PROCTOR	She only pretended to faint, Your Excellency. They're all marvellous pretenders.
HATHORNE	Then can she pretend to faint now?
PROCTOR	Now?
PARRIS	Why not? Now there are no spirits attacking her, for none in this room is accused of witchcraft. So let her turn herself cold now, let her pretend she is attacked now, let her faint. (*He turns to Mary Warren.*) Faint!

MARY   Faint?

PARRIS   Aye, faint. Prove to us how you pretended in the court so many times.

MARY   (*looking at Proctor*): I – cannot faint now, sir.

PROCTOR   (*alarmed, quietly*): Can you not pretend it?

MARY   I – (*she looks about as though searching for the passion to faint.*) I – have no *sense* of it now, I –

DANFORTH Why? What is lacking now?

MARY   I – cannot tell, sir, I –

DANFORTH Might it be that here we have no afflicting spirit loose, but in the court there were some?

MARY   I never saw no spirits.

PARRIS   Then see no spirits now, and prove to us that you can faint by your own will, as you claim.

MARY   (*stares, searching for the emotion of it, and then shakes her head*): I – cannot do it.

PARRIS   Then you will confess, will you not? It were attacking spirits made you faint!

MARY   No, sir, I –

PARRIS   Your Excellency, this is a trick to blind the court!

MARY   It's not a trick! (*She stands.*) I – I used to faint because I – I thought I saw spirits.

DANFORTH *Thought* you saw them!

MARY   But I did not, Your Honour.

HATHORNE How could you think you saw them unless you saw them?

MARY   I – I cannot tell how, but I did. I – I heard the other girls, screaming, and you, Your Honour, you seemed to believe them, and I – it were only sport in the beginning, sir, but then the whole world cried spirits, spirits, and I – I promise you, Mr Danforth, I only thought I saw them but I did not.

DANFORTH *peers at her.*

PARRIS   (*smiling, but nervous because* DANFORTH *seems to be struck by Mary Warren's story*): Surely Your Excellency is not taken by this simple lie.

DANFORTH	(*turning worriedly to Abigail*): Abigail. I bid you now search your heart and tell me this – and beware of it, child, to God every soul is precious and His vengeance is terrible on them that take life without cause. Is it possible, child, that the spirits you have seen are illusion only, some deception that may cross your mind when –
ABIGAIL	Why, this – this – is a base question, sir.
DANFORTH	Child, I would have you consider it –
ABIGAIL	I have been hurt, Mr Danforth; I have seen my blood runnin' out! I have been near to murdered every day because I done my duty pointing out the Devil's people – and this is my reward! To be mistrusted, denied, questioned like a –
DANFORTH	(*weakening*): Child, I do not mistrust you –
ABIGAIL	(*in an open threat*): Let *you* beware, Mr Danforth. Think you be so mighty that the power of Hell may not turn *your* wits? Beware of it! There is – (*Suddenly, from an accusatory attitude, her face turns, looking into the air above – it is truly frightened.*)
DANFORTH	(*apprehensively*): What is it, child?
ABIGAIL	(*looking about in the air, clasping her arms about her as though cold*): I – I know not. A wind, a cold wind, has come. (*Her eyes fall on Mary Warren.*)
MARY	(*terrified, pleading*): Abby!
MERCY	(*shivering*): Your Honour, I freeze!
PROCTOR	They're pretending!
HATHORNE	(*touching Abigail's hand*): She is cold, Your Honour, touch her!
MERCY	(*through chattering teeth*): Mary, do you send this shadow on me?
MARY	Lord, save me!
SUZANNA	I freeze, I freeze!
ABIGAIL	(*shivering visibly*): It is a wind, a wind!
MARY	Abby, don't do that!
DANFORTH	(*himself engaged and entered by Abigail*): Mary Warren, do you witch her? I say to you, do you send your spirit out?

With a hysterical cry MARY WARREN *starts to run.* PROCTOR *catches her.*

MARY   (*almost collapsing*): Let me go, Mr Proctor, I cannot, I cannot –

ABIGAIL   (*crying to Heaven*): Oh, Heavenly Father, take away this shadow!

Without warning or hesitation, PROCTOR *leaps at Abigail and, grabbing her by the hair pulls her to her feet. She screams in pain.* DANFORTH, *astonished, cries, 'What are you about?' and* HATHORNE *and* PARRIS *call, 'Take your hands off her!' and out of it all comes Proctor's roaring voice.*

PROCTOR   How do you call Heaven! Whore! Whore!

HERRICK *breaks Proctor from her.*

HERRICK   John!

DANFORTH   Man! Man, what do you –

PROCTOR   (*breathless and in agony*): It is a whore!

DANFORTH   (*dumbfounded*): You charge – ?

ABIGAIL   Mr Danforth, he is lying!

PROCTOR   Mark her! Now she'll suck a scream to stab me with, but –

DANFORTH   You will prove this! This will not pass!

PROCTOR   (*trembling, his life collapsing about him*): I have known her, sir. I have known her.

DANFORTH   You –you are a lecher?

FRANCIS   (*horrified*): John, you cannot say such a –

PROCTOR   Oh, Francis, I wish you had some evil in you that you might know me! (*To Danforth.*) A man will not cast away his good name. You surely know that.

DANFORTH   (*dumbfounded*): In – in what time? In what place?

PROCTOR   (*his voice about to break, and his shame great*): In the proper place – where my beasts are bedded. On the last night of my joy, some eight months past. She used to serve me in my house, sir. (*He has to clamp his jaw to keep from weeping.*) A man may think God sleeps but God sees everything, I know it now. I beg you, sir, I beg you – see her what she is. My wife, my dear good wife, took this girl soon after, sir, and put her out on the highroad. And being what she is, a lump of vanity, sir – (*He is being overcome.*) Excellency, forgive me, forgive me. (*Angrily against himself, he turns away from the Governor for a moment. Then, as though to cry is his only means of speech left.*) She thinks to dance with me on my wife's grave! And well she might, for I thought of her softly. God help me, I lusted, and there is a promise in such sweat. But it is a whore's vengeance, and you must see it; I set myself entirely in your hands. I know you must see it now.

DANFORTH (*blanched, in horror, turning to Abigail*): You deny every scrap and tittle of this?

ABIGAIL If I must answer that, I will leave and I will not come back again.

DANFORTH *seems unsteady.*

PROCTOR I have made a bell of my honour! I have rung the doom of my good name – you will believe me, Mr Danforth! My wife is innocent, except she knew a whore when she saw one!

ABIGAIL (*stepping up to Danforth*): What look do you give me? (DANFORTH *cannot speak.*) I'll not have such looks! (*She turns and starts for the door.*)

DANFORTH You will remain where you are! (HERRICK *steps into her path. She comes up short, fire in her eyes.*) Mr Parris, go into the court and bring Goodwife Proctor out.

PARRIS (*objecting*): Your Honour, this is all a –

DANFORTH (*sharply to Parris*): Bring her out! And tell her not one word of what's been spoken here. And let you knock before you enter. (PARRIS *goes out.*) Now we shall touch the bottom of this swamp. (*To Proctor.*) Your wife, you say, is an honest woman.

PROCTOR In her life, sir, she have never lied. There are them that cannot sing, and them that cannot weep – my wife cannot lie. I have paid much to learn it, sir.

DANFORTH And when she put this girl out of your house, she put her out for a harlot?

PROCTOR Aye, sir.

DANFORTH And knew her for a harlot?

PROCTOR   Aye, sir, she knew her for a harlot.

DANFORTH   Good then. (*To Abigail.*) And if she tell me, child, it were for harlotry, may God spread His mercy on you! (*There is a knock. He calls to the door.*) Hold! (*To Abigail.*) Turn your back. Turn your back. (*To Proctor.*) Do likewise. (*Both turn their backs – Abigail with indignant slowness.*) Now let neither of you turn to face Goody Proctor. No one in this room is to speak one word, or raise a gesture aye or nay. (*He turns toward the door, calls.*) Enter! (*The door opens.* ELIZABETH *enters with* PARRIS. PARRIS *leaves her. She stands alone, her eyes looking for Proctor.*) Mr Cheever, report this testimony in all exactness. Are you ready?

CHEEVER   Ready, sir.

DANFORTH   Come here, woman. (ELIZABETH *comes to him, glancing at Proctor's back.*) Look at me only, not at your husband. In my eyes only.

ELIZABETH   (*faintly*): Good, sir.

DANFORTH   We are given to understand that at one time you dismissed your servant, Abigail Williams.

ELIZABETH   That is true, sir.

DANFORTH   For what cause did you dismiss her? (*Slight pause. Then* ELIZABETH *tries to glance at Proctor.*) You will look in my eyes only and not at your husband. The answer is in your memory and you need no help to give it to me. Why did you dismiss Abigail Williams?

ELIZABETH   (*not knowing what to say, sensing a situation, wetting her lips to stall for time*): She – dissatisfied me. (*Pause.*) And my husband.

DANFORTH   In what way dissatisfied you?

ELIZABETH   She were – (*She glances at Proctor for a cue.*)

DANFORTH   Woman, look at me! (*Elizabeth does.*) Were she slovenly? Lazy? What disturbance did she cause?

ELIZABETH   Your Honour, I – in that time I were sick. And I – my husband is a good and righteous man. He is never drunk as some are, nor wastin' his time at the shovelboard, but always

	at his work. But in my sickness – you see, sir, I were a long time sick after my last baby, and I thought I saw my husband somewhat turning from me. And this girl – (*She turns to Abigail.*)
DANFORTH	Look at me.
ELIZABETH	Aye, sir. Abigail Williams – (*She breaks off.*)
DANFORTH	What of Abigail Williams?
ELIZABETH	I came to think he fancied her. And so one night I lost my wits, I think, and put her out on the highroad.
DANFORTH	Your husband – did he indeed turn from you?
ELIZABETH	(*in agony*): My husband – is a goodly man, sir.
DANFORTH	Then he did not turn from you.
ELIZABETH	(*starting to glance at Proctor*): He –
DANFORTH	(*reaches out and holds her face, then*): Look at me! To your own knowledge, has John Proctor ever committed the crime of lechery! (*In a crisis of indecision she cannot speak.*) Answer my question! Is your husband a lecher!
ELIZABETH	(*faintly*): No, sir.
DANFORTH	Remove her, Marshal.
PROCTOR	Elizabeth, tell the truth!
DANFORTH	She has spoken. Remove her!
PROCTOR	(*crying out*): Elizabeth, I have confessed it!
ELIZABETH	Oh, God! (*The door closes behind her.*)
PROCTOR	She only thought to save my name!
HALE	Excellency, it is a natural lie to tell: I beg you, stop now before another is condemned! I may shut my conscience to it no more – private vengeance is working through this testimony! From the beginning this man has struck me true. By my oath to Heaven, I believe him now, and pray you call back his wife before we –
DANFORTH	She spoke nothing of lechery, and this man has lied!
HALE	I believe him! (*Pointing to Abigail.*) This girl has always struck me false! She has –
	ABIGAIL, *with a weird, wild, chilling cry, screams up to the ceiling.*

ABIGAIL   You will not! Begone! Begone, I say!

DANFORTH   What is it, child? (*But* ABIGAIL, *pointing with fear, is now raising up her frightened eyes, her awed face, toward the ceiling – the girls are doing the same – and now* HATHORNE, HALE, PUTNAM, CHEEVER, HERRICK, *and* DANFORTH *do the same.*) What's there? (*He lowers his eyes from the ceiling, and now he is frightened; there is a real tension in his voice.*) Child! (*She is transfixed – with all the girls, she is whimpering open-mouthed, agape at the ceiling.*) Girls! Why do you – ?

MERCY   (*pointing*): It's on the beam! Behind the rafter!

DANFORTH   (*looking up*): Where!

ABIGAIL   Why – ? (*She gulps.*) Why do you come, yellow bird?

PROCTOR   Where's a bird? I see no bird!

ABIGAIL   (*to the ceiling*): My face? My face?

PROCTOR   Mr Hale –

DANFORTH   Be quiet!

PROCTOR   (*to Hale*): Do you see a bird?

DANFORTH   Be quiet!!

ABIGAIL   (*to the ceiling, in a genuine conversation with the 'bird' as though trying to talk it out of attacking her*): But God made my face; you cannot want to tear my face. Envy is a deadly sin, Mary.

MARY   (*on her feet with a spring, and horrified, pleading*): Abby!

ABIGAIL   (*unperturbed, continuing to the 'bird'*): Oh, Mary, this is a black art to change your shape. No, I cannot, I cannot stop my mouth; it's God's work I do.

MARY   Abby, I'm *here!*

PROCTOR   (*frantically*): They're pretending, Mr Danforth!

ABIGAIL   – (*now she takes a backward step, as though in fear the bird will swoop down momentarily*): Oh, please, Mary! Don't come down.

SUSANNA   Her claws, she's stretching her claws!

PROCTOR   Lies, lies.

ABIGAIL   (*backing further, eyes still fixed above*): Mary, please don't hurt me!

MARY	(*to Danforth*): I'm not hurting her!
DANFORTH	(*to Mary Warren*): Why does she see this vision?
MARY	She sees nothin'!
ABIGAIL	(*now staring full front as though hypnotized, and mimicking the exact tone of Mary Warren's cry*): She sees nothin'!
MARY	(*pleading*): Abby, you mustn't!
ABIGAIL AND ALL THE GIRLS	(*all transfixed*): Abby, you mustn't!
MARY	(*to all the girls*): I'm here, I'm here!
GIRLS	I'm here, I'm here!
DANFORTH	(*horrified*): Mary Warren! Draw back your spirit out of them!
MARY	Mr Danforth!
GIRLS	(*cutting her off*): Mr Danforth!
DANFORTH	Have you compacted with the Devil? Have you?
MARY	Never, never!
GIRLS	Never, never!
DANFORTH	(*growing hysterical*): Why can they only repeat you?
PROCTOR	Give me a whip – I'll stop it!
MARY	They're sporting. They – !
GIRLS	They're sporting!
MARY	(*turning to them all hysterically and stamping her feet*): Abby, stop it!
GIRLS	(*stamping their feet*): Abby, stop it!
MARY	Stop it!
GIRLS	Stop it!
MARY	(*screaming it out at the top of her lungs, and raising her fists*): Stop it!!
GIRLS	(*raising their fists*): Stop it!!
	MARY WARREN, *utterly confounded, and becoming overwhelmed by Agibail's – and the girls' – utter conviction, starts to whimper, hands half raised, powerless, and all the girls begin whimpering exactly as she does.*
DANFORTH	A little while ago you were afflicted. Now it seems you afflict others; where did you find this power?
MARY	(*staring at Abigail*): I – have no power.

GIRLS   I have no power.

PROCTOR   They're gulling you, Mister!

DANFORTH   Why did you turn about this past two weeks? You have seen the Devil, have you not?

HALE   (*indicating Abigail and the girls*): You cannot believe them!

MARY   I –

PROCTOR   (*sensing her weakening*): Mary, God damns all liars!

DANFORTH   (*pounding it into her*): You have seen the Devil, you have made compact with Lucifer, have you not?

PROCTOR   God damns liars, Mary!

MARY *utters something unintelligible, staring at Abigail, who keeps watching the 'bird' above.*

DANFORTH   I cannot hear you. What do you say? (MARY *utters again unintelligibly.*) You will confess yourself or you will hang! (*He turns her roughly to face him.*) Do you know who I am? I say you will hang if you do not open with me!

PROCTOR   Mary, remember the angel Raphael – do that which is good and –

ABIGAIL   (*pointing upwards*): The wings! Her wings are spreading! Mary, please, don't, don't – !

HALE   I see nothing, Your Honour!

DANFORTH   Do you confess this power! (*He is an inch from her face.*) Speak!

ABIGAIL   She's going to come down! She's walking the beam!

DANFORTH   Will you speak!

MARY   (*staring in horror*): I cannot!

GIRLS   I cannot!

PARRIS   Cast the Devil out! Look him in the face! Trample him! We'll save you, Mary, only stand fast against him and –

ABIGAIL   (*looking up*): Look out! She's coming down!

She and all the girls run to one wall, shielding their eyes. And now, as though cornered, they let out a gigantic scream, and MARY, *as though infected opens her mouth and screams with them. Gradually* ABIGAIL *and the* GIRLS *leave off, until only* MARY *is left there, staring up at the 'bird', screaming madly. All watch her, horrified by this evident fit.* PROCTOR *strides to her.*

PROCTOR   Mary, tell the Governor what they – (*He has hardly got a word out, when, seeing him coming for her, she rushes out of his reach, screaming in horror.*)

MARY   Don't touch me – don't touch me! (*At which the girls halt at the door.*)

PROCTOR   (*astonished*): Mary!

MARY   (*pointing at Proctor*): You're the Devil's man!

He is stopped in his tracks.

PARRIS   Praise God!

GIRLS   Praise God!

PROCTOR   (*numbed*): Mary, how – ?

MARY   I'll not hang with you! I love God, I love God.

DANFORTH   (*to Mary*): He bid you do the Devil's work?

MARY   (*hysterically, indicating Proctor*): He come at me by night and every day to sign, to sign, to –

DANFORTH   Sign what?

PARRIS   The Devil's book? He come with a book?

MARY   (*hysterically pointing at Proctor fearful of him*): My name, he want my name. 'I'll murder you,' he says, 'if my wife hangs! We must go and overthrow the court,' he says!

DANFORTH'S head jerks toward Proctor, shock and horror in his face.

PROCTOR   (*turning, appealing to Hale*): Mr Hale!

MARY   (*her sobs beginning*): He wake me every night, his eyes were like coals and his fingers claw my neck, and I sign, I sign . . .

HALE   Excellency, this child's gone wild!

PROCTOR   (*as Danforth's wide eyes pour on him*): Mary! Mary!

MARY   (*screaming at him*): No, I love God; I go your way no more. I love God, bless God. (*Sobbing, she rushes to Abigail.*) Abby, Abby, I'll never hurt you more! (*They all watch, as* ABIGAIL, *out of her infinite charity, reaches out and draws the sobbing Mary to her, and then looks up to Danforth.*)

DANFORTH   (*to Proctor*): What are you? (PROCTOR *is beyond speech in his anger.*) You are combined with anti-Christ, are you not? I have seen your power; you will not deny it! What say you, Mister?

HALE   Excellency –

DANFORTH   I will have nothing from you, Mr Hale! (*To Proctor.*) Will you confess yourself befouled with Hell, or do you keep that black allegiance yet? What say you?

PROCTOR   (*his mind wild, breathless*): I say – I say – God is dead!

PARRIS   Hear it, hear it!

PROCTOR   (*laughs insanely, then*): A fire, a fire is burning! I hear the boot of Lucifer, I see his filthy face! And it is my face, and yours, Danforth! For them that quail to bring men out of ignorance, as I have quailed, and as you quail now when you know in all your black hearts that this be fraud – God damns our kind especially, and we will burn, we will burn together!

DANFORTH   Marshal! Take him and Corey with him to the jail!

HALE   (*starting across to the door*): I denounce these proceedings!

PROCTOR   You are pulling Heaven down and raising up a whore!

HALE   I denounce these proceedings, I quit this court! (*He slams the door to the outside behind him.*)

DANFORTH   (*calling to him in a fury*): Mr Hale! Mr Hale!

THE CURTAIN FALLS

ACT FOUR

A cell in Salem jail, that fall.

At the back is a high barred window, near it, a great, heavy door.

Along the walls are two benches.

The place is in darkness but for the moonlight seeping through the bars. It appears empty. Presently footsteps are heard coming down a corridor beyond the wall, keys rattle, and the door swings open. MARSHAL HERRICK *enters with a lantern.*

He is nearly drunk, and heavy-footed. He goes to a bench and nudges a bundle of rags lying on it.

HERRICK	Sarah, wake up! Sarah Good! (*He then crosses to the other bench.*)
SARAH	(*rising in her rags*): Oh, Majesty! Comin', comin'! Tituba, he's here. His Majesty's come!
HERRICK	Go on to the north cell; this place is wanted now. (*He hangs his lantern on the wall.* TITUBA *sits up.*)
TITUBA	That don't look to me like His Majesty; look to me like the Marshal.
HERRICK	(*taking out a flask*): Get along with you now, clear this place. (*He drinks, and* SARAH GOOD *comes and peers up into his face.*)
SARAH	Oh, is it you, Marshal! I thought sure you be the devil comin' for us. Could I have a sip of cider for me goin' away?
HERRICK	(*handing her the flask*): And where are you off to, Sarah?
TITUBA	(*as Sarah drinks*): We goin' to Barbados, soon the Devil gits here with the feathers and the wings.
HERRICK	Oh? A happy voyage to you.
SARAH	A pair of bluebirds wingin' southerly, the two of us! Oh, it be a grand transformation, Marshal! (*She raises the flask to drink again.*)

HERRICK (*taking the flask from her lips*): You'd best give me that or you'll never rise off the ground. Come along now.

TITUBA I'll speak to him for you, if you desires to come along, Marshal.

HERRICK I'd not refuse it, Tituba; it's the proper morning to fly into Hell.

TITUBA Oh, it be no Hell in Barbados. Devil, him be pleasureman in Barbados, him be singin' and dancin' in Barbados. It's you folks – you riles him up 'round here; it be too cold 'round here for that Old Boy. He freeze his soul in Massachusetts, but in Barbados he just as sweet and – (*a bellowing cow is heard, and* TITUBA *leaps up and calls to the window.*) Aye, sir! That's him, Sarah!

SARAH I'm here, Majesty! (*They hurriedly pick up their rags as* HOPKINS, *a guard, enters.*)

HOPKINS The Deputy Governor's arrived.

HERRICK (*grabbing Tituba*): Come along, come along.

TITUBA (*resisting him*): No, he comin' for me. I goin' home!

HERRICK (*pulling her to the door*): That's not Satan, just a poor old cow with a hatful of milk. Come along now, out with you!

TITUBA (*calling to the window*): Take me home, Devil! Take me home!

SARAH (*following the shouting Tituba out*): Tell him I'm goin', Tituba! Now you tell him Sarah Good is goin' too!

In the corridor outside TITUBA *calls on –' Take me home, Devil; Devil, take me home!' and Hopkins' voice orders her to move on.* HERRICK *returns and begins to push old rags and straw into a corner. Hearing footsteps, he turns, and enter* DANFORTH *and* JUDGE HATHORNE. *They are in greatcoats and wear hats against the bitter cold. They are followed by* CHEEVER, *who carries a dispatch case and a flat wooden box containing his writing materials.*

HERRICK Good morning, Excellency.

DANFORTH Where is Mr Parris?

HERRICK I'll fetch him. (*He starts for the door.*)

DANFORTH	Marshal. (*Herrick stops.*) When did Reverend Hale arrive?
HERRICK	It were toward midnight, I think.
DANFORTH	(*suspiciously*): What is he about here?
HERRICK	He goes among them that will hang, sir. And he prays with them. He sits with Goody Nurse now. And Mr Parris with him.
DANFORTH	Indeed. That man have no authority to enter here, Marshal. Why have you let him in?
HERRICK	Why, Mr Parris command me, sir. I cannot deny him.
DANFORTH	Are you drunk, Marshal?
HERRICK	No, sir; it is a bitter night, and I have no fire here.
DANFORTH	(*containing his anger*): Fetch Mr Parris.
HERRICK	Aye, sir.
DANFORTH	There is a prodigious stench in this place.
HERRICK	I have only now cleared the people out for you.
DANFORTH	Beware hard drink, Marshal.
HERRICK	Aye, sir. (*He waits an instant for further orders. But* DANFORTH, *in dissatisfaction, turns his back on him, and* HERRICK *goes out. There is a pause,* DANFORTH *stands in thought.*)
HATHORNE	Let you question Hale, Excellency; I should not be surprised he have been preaching in Andover lately.
DANFORTH	We'll come to that; speak nothing of Andover. Parris prays with him. That's strange. (*He blows on his hands, moves toward the window, and looks out.*)
HATHORNE	Excellency, I wonder if it be wise to let Mr Parris so continuously with the prisoners. (DANFORTH *turns to him, interested.*) I think, sometimes, the man has a mad look these days.
DANFORTH	Mad?
HATHORNE	I met him yesterday coming out of his house, and I bid him good morning–and he wept and went his way. I think it is not well the village sees him so unsteady.
DANFORTH	Perhaps he have some sorrow.
CHEEVER	(*stamping his feet against the cold*): I think it be the cows, sir.

DANFORTH   Cows?

CHEEVER   There be so many cows wanderin' the highroads, now their masters are in the jails, and much disagreement who they will belong to now. I know Mr Parris be arguin' with farmers all yesterday – there is great contention, sir, about the cows. Contention make him weep, sir; it were always a man that weep for contention. (*He turns, as do* HATHORNE *and* DANFORTH *hearing someone coming up the corridor.* DANFORTH *raises his head as* PARRIS *enters. He is gaunt, frightened, and sweating in his greatcoat.*)

PARRIS   (*to Danforth, instantly*): Oh, good morning, sir, thank you for coming. I beg your pardon wakin' you so early. Good morning, Judge Hathorne.

DANFORTH   Reverend Hale have no right to enter this –

PARRIS   Excellency, a moment. (*He hurries back and shuts the door.*)

HATHORNE   Do you leave him alone with the prisoners?

DANFORTH   What's his business here?

PARRIS   (*prayerfully holding up his hands*): Excellency, hear me. It is a providence. Reverend Hale has returned to bring Rebecca Nurse to God.

DANFORTH   (*surprised*): He bids her confess?

PARRIS   (*sitting*): Hear me. Rebecca have not given me a word this three month since she came. Now she sits with him, and her sister and Martha Corey and two or three others, and he pleads with them, confess their crimes and save their lives.

DANFORTH   Why – this is indeed a providence. And they soften, they soften?

PARRIS   Not yet, not yet. But I thought to summon you, sir, that we might think on whether it be not wise, to – (*He dares not say it.*) I had thought to put a question, sir, and I hope you will not –

DANFORTH   Mr Parris, be plain, what troubles you?

PARRIS   There is news, sir, that the court – the court must reckon with. My niece, sir, my niece – I believe she has vanished.

DANFORTH   Vanished!

PARRIS	I had thought to advise you of it earlier in the week, but –
DANFORTH	Why? How long is she gone?
PARRIS	This be the third night. You see, sir, she told me she would stay a night with Mercy Lewis. And next day, when she does not return, I send to Mr Lewis to inquire. Mercy told him she would sleep in *my* house for a night.
DANFORTH	They are both gone?!
PARRIS	(*in fear of him*): They are, sir.
DANFORTH	(*alarmed*): I will send a party for them. Where may they be?
PARRIS	Excellency, I think they be aboard a ship. (DANFORTH *stands agape.*) My daughter tells me how she heard them speaking of ships last week, and tonight I discover my – my strongbox is broke into. (*He presses his fingers against his eyes to keep back tears.*)
HATHORNE	(*astonished*): She have robbed you?
PARRIS	Thirty-one pound is gone. I am penniless. (*He covers his face and sobs.*)
DANFORTH	Mr Parris, you are a brainless man! (*He walks in thought, deeply worried.*)
PARRIS	Excellency, it profit nothing you should blame me. I cannot think they would run off except they fear to keep in Salem any more. (*He is pleading.*) Mark it, sir, Abigail had close knowledge of the town, and since the news of Andover has broken here –
DANFORTH	Andover is remedied. The court returns there on Friday, and will resume examinations.
PARRIS	I am sure of it, sir. But the rumour here speaks rebellion in Andover, and it –
DANFORTH	There is no rebellion in Andover!
PARRIS	I tell you what is said here, sir. Andover have thrown out the court, they say, and will have no part of witchcraft. There be a faction here, feeding on that news, and I tell you true, sir, I fear there will be riot here.

HATHORNE Riot! Why, at every execution I have seen naught but high satisfaction in the town.

PARRIS Judge Hathorne – it were another sort that hanged till now. Rebecca Nurse is no Bridget that lived three year with Bishop before she married him. John Proctor is not Isaac Ward that drank his family to ruin. (*To Danforth.*) I would to God it were not so, Excellency, but these people have great weight yet in the town. Let Rebecca stand upon the gibbet and send up some righteous prayer, and I fear she'll wake a vengeance on you.

HATHORNE Excellency, she is condemned a witch. The court have –

DANFORTH (*in deep concern, raising a hand to Hathorne*): Pray you. (*To Parris.*) How do you propose, then?

PARRIS Excellency, I would postpone these hangin's for a time.

DANFORTH There will be no postponement.

PARRIS Now Mr Hale's returned, there is hope, I think – for if he brings even one of these to God, that confession surely damns the others in the public eye, and none may doubt more that they are all linked to Hell. This way, unconfessed and claiming innocence, doubts are multiplied, many honest people will weep for them, and our good purpose is lost in their tears.

DANFORTH (*after thinking a moment, then going to Cheever*): Give me the list.

CHEEVER *opens the dispatch case, searches.*

PARRIS It cannot be forgot, sir, that when I summoned the congregation for John Proctor's excommunication there were hardly thirty people come to hear it. That speak a discontent, I think, and –

DANFORTH (*studying the list*): There will be no postponement.

PARRIS Excellency –

DANFORTH Now, sir – which of these in your opinion may be brought to God? I will myself strive with him till dawn. (*He hands the list to* PARRIS, *who merely glances at it.*)

PARRIS	There is not sufficient time till dawn.
DANFORTH	I shall do my utmost. Which of them do you have hope for?
PARRIS	(*not even glancing at the list now, and in a quavering voice, quietly*): Excellency – a dagger – (*He chokes up.*)
DANFORTH	What do you say?
PARRIS	Tonight, when I open my door to leave my house – a dagger clattered to the ground. (*Silence.* DANFORTH *absorbs this. Now* PARRIS *cries out.*) You cannot hang this sort. There is danger for me. I dare not step outside at night!

REVEREND HALE *enters. They look at him for an instant in silence. He is steeped in sorrow, exhausted, and more direct than he ever was.*

DANFORTH	Accept my congratulations, Reverend Hale; we are gladdened to see you returned to your good work.
HALE	(*coming to Danforth now*): You must pardon them. They will not budge.

HERRICK *enters, waits.*

DANFORTH	(*conciliatory*): You misunderstand, sir; I cannot pardon these when twelve are already hanged for the same crime. It is not just.
PARRIS	(*with failing heart*): Rebecca will not confess?
HALE	The sun will rise in a few minutes. Excellency, I must have more time.
DANFORTH	Now hear me, and beguile yourselves no more. I will not receive a single plea for pardon or postponement. Them that will not confess will hang. Twelve are already executed; the names of these seven are given out, and the village expects to see them die this morning. Postponement now speaks a floundering on my part; reprieve or pardon must cast doubt upon the guilt of them that died till now. While I speak God's law, I will not crack its voice with whimpering. If retaliation is your fear, know this – I should hang ten thousand that dared to rise against the law, and an ocean of salt tears could not melt the resolution of the statutes. Now draw yourselves up like men and

help me, as you are bound by Heaven to do. Have you spoken with them all, Mr Hale?

HALE   All but Proctor. He is in the dungeon.

DANFORTH (*to Herrick*): What's Proctor's way now?

HERRICK He sits like some great bird; you'd not know he lived except he will take food from time to time.

DANFORTH (*after thinking a moment*): His wife – his wife must be well on with child now.

HERRICK She is, sir.

DANFORTH What think you, Mr Parris? You have closer knowledge of this man; might her presence soften him?

PARRIS   It is possible, sir. He have not laid eyes on her these three months. I should summon her.

DANFORTH (*to Herrick*): Is he yet adamant? Has he struck at you again?

HERRICK He cannot, sir, he is chained to the wall now.

DANFORTH (*after thinking on it*): Fetch Goody Proctor to me. Then let you bring him up.

HERRICK Aye, sir. (HERRICK *goes. There is silence.*)

HALE   Excellency, if you postpone a week and publish to the town that you are striving for their confessions, that speak mercy on your part, not faltering.

DANFORTH Mr Hale, as God have not empowered me like Joshua to stop this sun from rising, so I cannot withhold from them the perfection of their punishment.

HALE   (*harder now*): If you think God wills you to raise rebellion, Mr Danforth, you are mistaken!

DANFORTH (*instantly*): You have heard rebellion spoken in the town?

HALE   Excellency, there are orphans wandering from house to house; abandoned cattle bellow on the highroads, the stink of rotting crops hangs everywhere, and no man knows when the harlot's cry will end his life – and you wonder yet if rebellion's spoke? Better you should marvel how they do not burn your province!

DANFORTH	Mr Hale, have you preached in Andover this month?
HALE	Thank God they have no need of me in Andover.
DANFORTH	You baffle me, sir. Why have you returned here?
HALE	Why, it is all simple. I come to do the Devil's work. I come to counsel Christians they should belie themselves. (*His sarcasm collapses.*) There is blood on my head! Can you not see the blood on my head?
PARRIS	Hush! (*For he has heard footsteps. They all face the door.* HERRICK *enters with* ELIZABETH. *Her wrists are linked by heavy chain, which* HERRICK *now removes. Her clothes are dirty; her face is pale and gaunt.* HERRICK *goes out.*)
DANFORTH	(*very politely*): Goody Proctor. (*She is silent.*) I hope you are hearty?
ELIZABETH	(*as a warning reminder*): I am yet six month before my time.
DANFORTH	Pray be at your ease, we come not for your life. We – (*uncertain how to plead, for he is not accustomed to it.*) Mr Hale, will you speak with the woman?
HALE	Goody Proctor, your husband is marked to hang this morning.
	Pause.
ELIZABETH	(*quietly*): I have heard it.
HALE	You know, do you not, that I have no connection with the court? (*She seems to doubt it.*) I come of my own, Goody Proctor. I would save your husband's life, for if he is taken I count myself his murderer. Do you understand me?
ELIZABETH	What do you want of me?
HALE	Goody Proctor, I have gone this three month like our Lord into the wilderness. I have sought a Christian way, for damnation's doubled on a minister who counsels men to lie.
HATHORNE	It is no lie, you cannot speak of lies.
HALE	It is a lie! They are innocent!
DANFORTH	I'll hear no more of that!
HALE	(*continuing to Elizabeth*): Let you not mistake your duty

as I mistook my own. I came into this village like a bridegroom to his beloved, bearing gifts of high religion; the very crowns of holy law I brought, and what I touched with my bright confidence, it died; and where I turned the eye of my great faith, blood flowed up. Beware, Goody Proctor – cleave to no faith when faith brings blood. It is mistaken law that leads you to sacrifice. Life, woman, life is God's most precious gift; no principle, however glorious, may justify the taking of it. I beg you, woman, prevail upon your husband to confess. Let him give his lie. Quail not before God's judgement in this, for it may well be God damns a liar less than he that throws his life away for pride. Will you plead with him? I cannot think he will listen to another.

ELIZABETH (*quietly*): I think that be the Devil's argument.

HALE (*with a climactic desperation*): Woman, before the laws of God we are as swine! We cannot read His will!

ELIZABETH I cannot dispute with you, sir; I lack learning for it.

DANFORTH (*going to her*): Goody Proctor, you are not summoned here for disputation. Be there no wifely tenderness within you? He will die with the sunrise. Your husband. Do you understand it? (*She only looks at him.*) What say you? Will you contend with him? (*She is silent.*) Are you stone? I tell you true, woman, had I no other proof of your unnatural life, your dry eyes now would be sufficient evidence that you delivered up your soul to Hell! A very ape would weep at such calamity! Have the devil dried up any tear of pity in you? (*She is silent.*) Take her out. It profit nothing she should speak to him!

ELIZABETH (*quietly*): Let me speak with him, Excellency.

PARRIS (*with hope*): You'll strive with him? (*She hesitates.*)

DANFORTH Will you plead for his confession or will you not?

ELIZABETH I promise nothing. Let me speak with him.

A sound – the sibilance of dragging feet on stone. They turn. A pause. HERRICK *enters with* JOHN PROCTOR. *His wrists are chained.*

He is another man, bearded, filthy, his eyes misty as though webs had overgrown them. He halts inside the doorway, his eye caught by the sight of Elizabeth. The emotion flowing between them prevents anyone from speaking for an instant. Now HALE, *visibly affected, goes to Danforth and speaks quietly.*

HALE Pray, leave them, Excellency.

DANFORTH (*pressing Hale impatiently aside*): Mr Proctor, you have been notified, have you not? (PROCTOR *is silent, staring at Elizabeth.*) I see light in the sky, Mister; let you counsel with your wife, and may God help you turn your back on Hell. (PROCTOR *is silent, staring at Elizabeth.*)

HALE (*quietly*): Excellency, let –

DANFORTH *brushes past Hale and walks out.* HALE *follows.* CHEEVER *stands and follows,* HATHORNE *behind.* HERRICK *goes.* PARRIS, *from a safe distance, offers:*

PARRIS If you desire a cup of cider, Mr Proctor, I am sure I – (PROCTOR *turns an icy stare at him, and he breaks off.* PARRIS *raises his palms towards Proctor.*) God lead you now. (PARRIS *goes out.*)

Alone, PROCTOR *walks to her, halts. It is as though they stood in a spinning world. It is beyond sorrow, above it. He reaches out his hand as though toward an embodiment not quite real, and as he touches her, a strange soft sound, half laughter, half amazement, comes from his throat. He pats her hand. She covers his hand with hers. And then, weak, he sits. Then she sits, facing him.*

PROCTOR The child?

ELIZABETH It grows.

PROCTOR There is no word of the boys?

ELIZABETH They're well. Rebecca's Samuel keeps them.

PROCTOR You have not seen them?

ELIZABETH I have not. (*She catches a weakening in herself and downs it.*)

PROCTOR You are a – marvel, Elizabeth.

ELIZABETH You – have been tortured?

PROCTOR Aye. (*Pause. She will not let herself be drowned in the sea that threatens her.*) They come for my life now.

ELIZABETH	I know it.
	Pause.
PROCTOR	None – have yet confessed?
ELIZABETH	There be many confessed.
PROCTOR	Who are they?
ELIZABETH	There be a hundred or more, they say. Goody Ballard is one; Isaiah Goodkind is one. There be many.
PROCTOR	Rebecca?
ELIZABETH	Not Rebecca. She is one foot in Heaven now; naught may hurt her more.
PROCTOR	And Giles?
ELIZABETH	You have not heard of it?
PROCTOR	I hear nothin', where I am kept.
ELIZABETH	Giles is dead.
	He looks at her incredulously.
PROCTOR	When were he hanged?
ELIZABETH	(*quietly, factually*): He were not hanged. He would not answer aye or nay to his indictment; for if he denied the charge they'd hang him surely, and auction out his property. So he stand mute, and died Christian under the law. And so his sons will have his farm. It is the law, for he could not be condemned a wizard without he answer the indictment, aye or nay.
PROCTOR	Then how does he die?
ELIZABETH	(*gently*): They press him, John.
PROCTOR	Press?
ELIZABETH	Great stones they lay upon his chest until he please aye or nay. (*With a tender smile for the old man.*) They say he give them but two words. 'More weight,' he says. And died.
PROCTOR	(*numbed – a thread to weave into his agony*): 'More weight'.
ELIZABETH	Aye. It were a fearsome man, Giles Corey.
	Pause.
PROCTOR	(*with great force of will, but not quite looking at her*): I have been thinking I would confess to them, Elizabeth. (*She shows nothing.*) What say you? If I give them that?

ELIZABETH	I cannot judge you, John.
	Pause.
PROCTOR	(*simply – a pure question*): What would you have me do?
ELIZABETH	As you will, I would have it. (*Slight pause.*) I want you living, John. That's sure.
PROCTOR	(*pauses, then with a flailing of hope*): Giles' wife? Have she confessed?
ELIZABETH	She will not.
	Pause.
PROCTOR	It is a pretence, Elizabeth.
ELIZABETH	What is?
PROCTOR	I cannot mount the gibbet like a saint. It is a fraud. I am not that man. (*She is silent.*) My honesty is broke, Elizabeth; I am no good man. Nothing's spoiled by giving them this lie that were not rotten long before.
ELIZABETH	And yet you've not confessed till now. That speak goodness in you.
PROCTOR	Spite only keeps me silent. It is hard to give a lie to dogs. (*Pause, for the first time he turns directly to her.*) I would have your forgiveness, Elizabeth.
ELIZABETH	It is not for me to give, John, I am –
PROCTOR	I'd have you see some honesty in it. Let them that never lied die now to keep their souls. It is pretence for me, a vanity that will not blind God nor keep my children out of the wind. (*Pause.*) What say you?
ELIZABETH	(*upon a heaving sob that always threatens*): John, it come to naught that I should forgive you, if you'll not forgive yourself. (*Now he turns away a little, in great agony.*) It is not my soul, John, it is yours. (*He stands, as though in physical pain, slowly rising to his feet with a great immortal longing to find his answer. It is difficult to say, and she is on the verge of tears.*) Only be sure of this, for I know it now: Whatever you will do, it is a good man does it. (*He turns his doubting, searching gaze upon her.*) I have read my heart this three months, John. (*Pause.*) I have sins of my own to count. It needs a cold wife to prompt lechery.

PROCTOR   (*in great pain*): Enough, enough –

ELIZABETH   (*now pouring out her heart*): Better you should know me!

PROCTOR   I will not hear it! I know you!

ELIZABETH   You take my sins upon you, John –

PROCTOR   (*in agony*): No, I take my own, my own!

ELIZABETH   John, I counted myself so plain, so poorly made, no honest love could come to me! Suspicion kissed you when I did; I never knew how I should say my love. It were a cold house I kept! (*In fright, she swerves, as* HATHORNE *enters.*)

HATHORNE   What say you Proctor? The sun is soon up.

PROCTOR, *his chest heaving, stares, turns to Elizabeth. She comes to him as though to plead, her voice quaking.*

ELIZABETH   Do what you will. But let none be your judge. There be no higher judge under Heaven than Proctor is! Forgive me, forgive me, John – I never knew such goodness in the world! (*She covers her face, weeping.*)

PROCTOR *turns from her to Hathorne; he is off the earth, his voice hollow.*

PROCTOR   I want my life.

HATHORNE   (*electrified, surprised*): You'll confess yourself?

PROCTOR   I will have my life.

HATHORNE   (*with a mystical tone*): God be praised! It is a providence! (*He rushes out the door, and his voice is heard calling down the corridor*): He will confess! Proctor will confess!

PROCTOR   (*with a cry, as he strides to the door*): Why do you cry it? (*In great pain he turns back to her.*) It is evil, is it not? It is evil.

ELIZABETH   (*in terror, weeping*): I cannot judge you, John, I cannot!

PROCTOR   Then who will judge me? (*Suddenly clasping his hands.*) God in Heaven, what is John Proctor, what is John Proctor? (*He moves as an animal, and a fury is riding in him, a tantalized search.*) I think it is honest, I think so; I am no saint. (*As though she had denied this he calls angrily at her.*) Let Rebecca go like a saint; for me it is fraud!

Voices are heard in the hall, speaking together in suppressed excitement.

ELIZABETH   I am not your judge, I cannot be. (*As though giving him release.*) Do as you will, do as you will!

PROCTOR   Would you give them such a lie? Say it. Would you ever give them this? (*She cannot answer.*) You would not; if tongs of fire were singeing you you would not! It is evil. Good, then – it is evil, and I do it!

HATHORNE *enters with* DANFORTH, *and, with them,* CHEEVER, PARRIS, *and* HALE. *It is a businesslike, rapid entrance, as though the ice had been broken.*

DANFORTH   (*with great relief and gratitude*): Praise to God, man, praise to God; you shall be blessed in Heaven for this. (CHEEVER *has hurried to the bench with pen, ink, and paper.* PROCTOR *watches him.*) Now then, let us have it. Are you ready, Mr Cheever?

PROCTOR   (*with a cold, cold horror at their efficiency*): Why must it be written?

DANFORTH   Why, for the good instruction of the village, Mister; this we shall post upon the church door! (*To Parris, urgently.*) Where is the marshal?

PARRIS   (*runs to the door and calls down the corridor*): Marshal! Hurry!

DANFORTH   Now, then, Mister, will you speak slowly, and directly to the point, for Mr Cheever's sake. (*He is on record now, and is really dictating to* CHEEVER, *who writes.*) Mr Proctor, have you seen the Devil in your life? (PROCTOR'S *jaws lock.*) Come man, there is light in the sky; the town waits at the scaffold; I would give out this news. Did you see the Devil?

PROCTOR   I did.

PARRIS   Praise God!

DANFORTH   And when he come to you, what were his demand? (PROCTOR *is silent.* DANFORTH *helps.*) Did he bid you to do his work upon the earth?

PROCTOR   He did.

DANFORTH   And you bound yourself to his service? (DANFORTH *turns, as* REBECCA *enters, with* HERRICK *helping to support her. She is barely able to walk.*) Come in, come in, woman!

REBECCA   (*brightening as she sees Proctor*): Ah, John! You are well, then, eh?

PROCTOR *turns his face to the wall.*

DANFORTH   Courage, man, courage – let her witness your good example that she may come to God herself. Now hear it, Goody Nurse! Say on, Mr Proctor. Did you bind yourself to the Devil's service?

REBECCA   (*astonished*): Why, John!

PROCTOR   (*through his teeth, his face turned from Rebecca*): I did.

DANFORTH   Now, woman, you surely see it profit nothin' to keep this conspiracy any further. Will you confess yourself with him?

REBECCA: Oh, John – God send his mercy on you!

DANFORTH   I say, will you confess yourself, Goody Nurse?

REBECCA   Why, it is a lie, it is a lie; how may I damn myself? I cannot, I cannot.

DANFORTH   Mr Proctor. When the Devil came to you did you see Rebecca Nurse in his company? (PROCTOR *is silent.*) Come, man, take courage – did you ever see her with the Devil?

PROCTOR   (*almost inaudibly*): No.

DANFORTH *now sensing trouble, glances at John and goes to the table, and picks up a sheet – the list of condemned.*

DANFORTH   Did you ever see her sister, Mary Easty, with the Devil?

PROCTOR   No, I did not.

DANFORTH   (*his eyes narrow on Proctor*): Did you ever see Martha Corey with the Devil?

PROCTOR   I did not.

DANFORTH   (*realizing, slowly putting the sheet down*): Did you ever see anyone with the Devil?

PROCTOR   I did not.

DANFORTH	Proctor, you mistake me. I am not empowered to trade your life for a lie. You have most certainly seen some person with the Devil. (PROCTOR *is silent.*) Mr Proctor, a score of people have already testified they saw this woman with the Devil.
PROCTOR	Then it is proved. Why must I say it?
DANFORTH	Why 'must' you say it! Why, you should rejoice to say it if your soul if truly purged of any love for Hell!
PROCTOR	They think to go like saints. I like not to spoil their names.
DANFORTH	(*inquiring, incredulously*): Mr Proctor, do you think they go like saints?
PROCTOR	(*evading*): This woman never thought she done the Devil's work.
DANFORTH	Look you, sir. I think you mistake your duty here. It matters nothing what she thought – she is convicted of the unnatural murder of children, and you for sending your spirit out upon Mary Warren. Your soul alone is the issue here, Mister, and you will prove its whiteness or you cannot live in a Christian country. Will you tell me now what persons conspired with you in the Devil's company? (PROCTOR *is silent.*) To your knowledge was Rebecca Nurse ever –
PROCTOR	I speak my own sins; I cannot judge another. (*Crying out, with hatred.*) I have no tongue for it.
HALE	(*quickly to Danforth*): Excellency, it is enough he confess himself. Let him sign it, let him sign it.
PARRIS	(*feverishly*): It is a great service, sir. It is a weighty name; it will strike the village that Proctor confess. I beg you, let him sign it. The sun is up, Excellency!
DANFORTH	(*considers; then with dissatisfaction*): Come, then, sign your testimony. (*To Cheever.*) Give it to him. (CHEEVER *goes to Proctor, the confession and a pen in hand.* PROCTOR *does not look at it.*) Come, man, sign it.
PROCTOR	(*after glancing at the confession*): You have all witnessed it – it is enough.

DANFORTH   You will not sign it?

PROCTOR   You have all witnessed it; what more is needed?

DANFORTH   Do you sport with me? You will sign your name or it is no confession, Mister! (*His breast heaving with agonized breathing,* PROCTOR *now lays the paper down and signs his name.*)

PARRIS   Praise be to the Lord!

PROCTOR *has just finished signing when* DANFORTH *reaches for the paper. But* PROCTOR *snatches it up, and now a wild terror is rising in him, and a boundless anger.*

DANFORTH   (*perplexed, but politely extending his hand*): If you please, sir.

PROCTOR   No.

DANFORTH   (*as though Proctor did not understand*): Mr Proctor, I must have –

PROCTOR   No, no, I have signed it. You have seen me. It is done! You have no need for this.

PARRIS   Proctor, the village must have proof that –

PROCTOR   Damn the village! I confess to God, and God has seen my name on this! It is enough!

DANFORTH   No, sir, it is –

PROCTOR   You came to save my soul, did you not? Here! I have confessed myself; it is enough!

DANFORTH   You have not con –

PROCTOR   I have confessed myself! Is there no good penitence but it be public? God does not need my name nailed upon the church! God sees my name; God knows how black my sins are! It is enough!

DANFORTH   Mr Proctor –

PROCTOR   You will not use me! I am no Sarah Good or Tituba, I am John Proctor! You will not use me! It is no part of salvation that you should use me!

DANFORTH   I do not wish to –

PROCTOR   I have three children – how may I teach them to walk like men in the world, and I sold my friends?

DANFORTH   You have not sold your friends –

PROCTOR   Beguile me not! I blacken all of them when this is nailed to the church the very day they hang for silence!

DANFORTH   Mr Proctor, I must have good and legal proof that you –

PROCTOR   You are the high court, your word is good enough! Tell them I confessed myself; say Proctor broke his knees and wept like a woman; say what you will, but my name cannot –

DANFORTH   (*with suspicion*): It is the same, is it not? If I report it or you sign to it?

PROCTOR   – (*he knows it is insane*): No, it is not the same! What others say and what I sign to is not the same!

DANFORTH   Why? Do you mean to deny this confession when you are free?

PROCTOR   I mean to deny nothing!

DANFORTH   Then explain to me, Mr Proctor, why you will not let –

PROCTOR   (*with a cry of his whole soul*): Because it is my name! Because I cannot have another in my life! Because I lie and sign myself to lies! Because I am not worth the dust on the feet of them that hang! How may I live without my name? I have given you my soul; leave me my name!

DANFORTH   (*pointing at the confession in Proctor's hand*): Is that document a lie? If it is a lie I will not accept it! What say you? I will not deal in lies, Mister! (PROCTOR *is motionless.*) You will give me your honest confession in my hand, or I cannot keep you from the rope. (PROCTOR *does not reply.*) Which way do you go, Mister?

His breast heaving, his eyes staring, PROCTOR *tears the paper and crumples it, and he is weeping in fury, but erect.*

DANFORTH   Marshal!

PARRIS   (*hysterically, as though the tearing paper were his life*): Proctor, Proctor!

HALE   Man, you will hang! You cannot!

PROCTOR   (*his eyes full of tears*): I can. And there's your first marvel, that I can. You have made your magic now, for now

I do think I see some shred of goodness in John Proctor. Not enough to weave a banner with, but white enough to keep it from such dogs. (ELIZABETH, *in a burst of terror, rushes to him and weeps against his hand.*) Give them no tear! Tears pleasure them! Show honour now, show a stony heart and sink them with it! (*He has lifted her, and kisses her now with great passion.*)

REBECCA Let you fear nothing! Another judgement waits us all!

DANFORTH Hang them high over the town! Who weeps for these, weeps for corruption! (*He sweeps out past them.* HERRICK *starts to lead* REBECCA, *who almost collapses, but* PROCTOR *catches her, and she glances up at him apologetically.*)

REBECCA I've had no breakfast.

HERRICK Come, man.

HERRICK escorts them out, HATHORNE *and* CHEEVER *behind them.* ELIZABETH *stands staring at the empty doorway.*

PARRIS (*in deadly fear, to Elizabeth*): Go to him, Goody Proctor! There is yet time!

From outside a drumroll strikes the air. PARRIS *is startled.* ELIZABETH *jerks about towards the window.*

PARRIS Go to him! (*He rushes out the door, as though to hold back his fate.*) Proctor! Proctor!

Again, a short burst of drums.

HALE Woman, plead with him! (*He starts to rush out the door, and then goes back to her.*) Woman! It is pride, it is vanity. (*She avoids his eyes, and moves to the window. He drops to his knees.*) Be his helper! – What profits him to bleed? Shall the dust praise him? Shall the worms declare his truth? Go to him, take his shame away!

ELIZABETH (*supporting herself against collapse, grips the bars of the window, and with a cry*): He have his goodness now. God forbid I take it from him!

The final drumroll crashes, then heightens violently. HALE *weeps in frantic prayer, and the new sun is pouring in upon her face, and the drums rattle like bones in the morning air.*

THE CURTAIN FALLS

ECHOES DOWN THE CORRIDOR

Not long after the fever died, Parris was voted from office, walked out on the highroad, and was never heard of again.

The legend has it that Abigail turned up later as a prostitute in Boston.

Twenty years after the last execution, the government awarded compensation to the victims still living, and to the families of the dead. However, it is evident that some people still were unwilling to admit their total guilt, and also that the factionalism was still alive, for some beneficiaries were actually not victims at all, but informers.

Elizabeth Proctor married again, four years after Proctor's death.

In solemn meeting, the congregation rescinded the excommunications – this in March 1712. But they did so upon orders of the government. The jury, however, wrote a statement praying forgiveness of all who had suffered.

Certain farms which had belonged to the victims were left to ruin, and for more than a century no one would buy them or live on them.

To all intents and purposes, the power of theocracy in Massachusetts was broken.

QUESTIONS AND EXPLORATIONS

1 Keeping Track

Act One

1 In what state of mind is Parris when we first meet him?

2 What condition is Betty in?

3 What has brought about Betty's condition?

4 Why is Parris so concerned that the villagers should not know what Abigail and Betty have been doing?

5 What did Parris actually see going on in the forest?

6 What is Abigail's explanation for leaving the Proctors' service and for finding no work since?

7 What is Ruth Putnam's condition?

8 How was Mrs Putnam involved in the events in the forest?

9 What do we learn after the adults leave the room about what the girls were doing the previous evening?

10 How does Abigail threaten the other girls to make them keep silent?

11 What do we gather about the previous relationship between Abigail and Proctor?

12 How does Rebecca Nurse explain the children's strange behaviour?

13 What reasons does John Proctor give for staying away from church?

14 What evidence is there that Parris is unhappy with the way he is treated by his congregation?

15 What is the argument about lumber (wood) between Proctor and Putnam?

16 Why has the Reverend Hale come to Salem? What does he hope to do?

17 What more do we learn about events in the forest from Hale's questioning of Abigail?

18 What does Tituba add to this story?

19 What does Hale want Tituba to confess? How does he achieve this?

20 What do the girls do in the last few minutes of Act One?

Act Two

1 How much time has passed since the end of Act One?

2 Describe what Elizabeth is doing, off-stage, when John comes home.

3 Why does John put extra salt in the stew?

4 What has John been doing during the day?

5 How does John 'mean to please' Elizabeth?

6 What was Mary Warren's explanation for leaving the house and going into Salem that day?

7 Why does Elizabeth think that John should go to Ezekiel Cheever?

8 What makes her suspicious about John's behaviour?

9 Why does John regret that he told Elizabeth about his affair with Abigail?

10 What news does Mary Warren bring from town?

11 What had Mary Warren to do with the accusing of Goody Osburn?

12 What makes the Reverend Hale suspicious that John and Elizabeth are not good Christians?

13 John cannot remember the commandment about adultery. Explain the stage direction 'as though a secret arrow had pained his heart'.

14 What is Hale's reaction when John tells him that Abigail and the girls had 'naught to do with witchcraft'?

15 What is Ezekiel Cheever's task on this particular night?

16 What happened to Abigail while she was at dinner?

17 What is Mary's explanation for the poppet having a needle stuck in it?

18 What does Proctor particularly object to about the way the women are arrested and held?

19 What advice does Hale leave with Proctor, Giles, Corey and Francis Nurse?

20 Why does Mary feel that she cannot tell the court what she knows about Abigail?

Act Three

1 Describe what the audience sees and hears when the scene begins.

2 Why have Giles Corey and Francis Nurse come to intervene in the court proceedings?

3 Why has John Proctor brought Mary Warren in the court?

4 What is Parris's opinion of John Proctor's actions?

5 How does Mary Warren explain her behaviour and that of Abigail and the other girls?

6 What does Proctor say is his reason for coming to the court?

7   What evidence is there that John Proctor does not appear to be a good Christian?

8   How does he react to the news that his wife is pregnant?

9   Why, in spite of the fact that his wife is 'temporarily' saved, does John Proctor persist in trying to give evidence?

10   Why does Danforth say that all the people who signed the testament should come to court?

11   What is Giles' evidence that Mr Putnam is using the court for his own purposes?

12   How does Danforth explain the importance of the victims' testifying in a trial for witchcraft?

13   What is Mary Warren's explanation for having changed her mind now?

14   How does Abigail's story about the poppet in Proctor's house differ from the version we heard earlier?

15   What evidence does John Proctor give to contradict Abigail's version of events?

16   How does Mary's explanation that earlier she had been pretending come to nothing?

17   Why is Mary frightened by the behaviour of Abigail and the other girls?

18   What does Proctor accuse Abigail of in order to silence her?

19   Explain how Danforth uses Elizabeth to test the truth of John's accusation against Abigail.

20   What does Abigail do which wins Mary back to her at the end of the scene?

Act Four

1   What do Sarah Good and Tituba think is going to happen to them?

2 Why does Marshal Herrick need to clear the cell?

3 Why does the Reverend Hale visit the prison?

4 How does Cheever explain Parris's sorrow and 'mad look'?

5 What news does Parris bring about Abigail and Mercy Lewis?

6 What has happened recently in the neighbouring village of Andover?

7 What is Danforth's reasoning for refusing to pardon or postpone the execution of the prisoners?

8 Why do they propose bringing Elizabeth to see John?

9 What is the condition of Salem and its farms since so many villagers have been either jailed or executed?

10 How does Hale try to persuade Elizabeth to try to save John's life?

11 How does Danforth try with the same intention?

12 How do Elizabeth and John greet each other?

13 What has happened to Giles Corey? Why did he refuse to answer the charge against him?

14 What is Proctor's reason for confessing now – just before the time of his execution?

15 What is Elizabeth's opinion of her husband?

16 Why is John so reluctant first of all to dictate his confession and then to sign it?

17 What makes Danforth suspicious of this confession?

18 Why does Danforth refuse after all to accept John's confession?

19 Why do Hale and Parris both urge Elizabeth to plead with John at the last moment?

20 What information is given us in the postscript 'Echoes Down the Corridor'?

2 Explorations

The questions in this section ask for your opinions on characters in the play from what they say and do. Always try to support your opinion with evidence from the text.

A Characters

John Proctor

1 What is your impression of the relationship between Proctor and Abigail from what we see of them together at the beginning of Act One.

2 Look again at the beginning of Act Two. How does the playwright show the audience the strain in the relationship between John and Elizabeth Proctor?

3 By the interval (say between Acts Two and Three) what impression do you have of John Proctor? What do you think he will do now, and why?

4 In Act Three Danforth tells Proctor that his wife's life is saved for another year because she is expecting a child. What are the various courses of action open to Proctor at this point? Why does he pursue the one he does?

5 On page 109 Proctor says, 'I cannot mount the gibbet like a saint. It is a fraud. I am not that man.' At the end of the play he goes to execution saying, 'now I do think I see some shred of goodness in John Proctor'.
What has made this change come about?

Elizabeth Proctor

1 Both John Proctor and Abigail call Elizabeth 'cold'. What evidence do you see in the play of this coldness? What does Elizabeth say about it and why?

2 In order to save her husband's life, Elizabeth tells a lie in Act Three. How does the playwright make this incident dramatic?

3 Look again at Act Four when Elizabeth and John Proctor meet again in the prison. Do you see any changes in their relationship?

4 Why does Elizabeth refuse to promise Danforth that she will try to persuade John to confess? What is her attitude towards John at the very end of the play?

5 If you were directing this play, what advice would you give to the actress playing Elizabeth about her character and development? What evidence would support this advice?

6 Imagine that you could interview Elizabeth after the birth of her fourth child. What particular questions would you want to ask her and why?

Abigail Williams

1 Look at what happened to Abigail before the play begins and at her circumstances at the beginning of the play. Does what you have discovered explain her behaviour?

2 Look again at Act One and note the way Abigail speaks to Parris and to the other girls. What impression do you have of her?

3 At the end of Act Three, Mary Warren is defeated by Abigail and once more takes her side. How does Abigail exert her power over Mary in this scene?

4 Why do you think Abigail leaves Salem and steals her uncle's money? Why doesn't she stay to see the result of the court's work?

5 Do you have any sympathy for Abigail? Give evidence for your opinion.

6 Do you think that Abigail alone was responsible for the Salem witch-trials or did the blame lie with other people or situations?

7 Imagine that you are Abigail long after these events have happened. Write your own account of the court proceedings and try to explain why you behaved as you did.

8 What is the importance of Abigail in the progress of the play?

John Hale

1 Look at the scene in which Hale first comes to Salem with his learned books. What kind of a man is he and what are his hopes?
Now look at Hale in Act Four. How has he changed and why?

2 In Act Two, Hale visits John and Elizabeth Proctor in their home. Why does he make this visit? What impression do you have of him in this scene?

Danforth

1 Look at Act Three at the scene in which Danforth tests Elizabeth's loyalty to her husband. Why does he ignore Hale's plea that 'it is a natural lie to tell'? What do you think is the importance of this scene?

2 In the prison scene, Act Four, Danforth insists that he

cannot postpone the executions because it would appear to be 'a floundering on my part'. From this speech and from other evidence in the play about Danforth, what do you think his attitude is towards justice and mercy?

Parris

1 By the end of the play, Parris is clearly a changed man. Discuss the various steps of this change and try to explain why they happened.

Minor Characters

1 Imagine that you are Mary Warren. Write a diary noting what happens each day and how you feel about events in the village and the court and the fates of people you know.

2 What is the importance of Ezekiel Cheever to this story? Find out exactly what he does and how it influences other people's lives.

3 You are the mother of the family which looks after John and Elizabeth's three children until Elizabeth is released from prison. How do you explain to these children what is happening to their parents?

4 Francis Nurse tried to secure the release of his wife Rebecca with a document signed by many villagers testifying to her good name. Imagine that you are Francis going from house to house. How would you persuade people to sign?

5 What part did the Putnams play in these events? Do you attach any blame to them or do you sympathise with them? Give good evidence for your opinions.

6 Look again at what Judge Hathorne does and says. Is he a distinctive character in his own right or merely a close follower of Danforth?

B Themes

The individual and society

1 Find all the evidence you can in the text showing the pressures on individual men to conform to what society expects of them. Why does it seem so important to the other characters, for example, that John Proctor had not been a regular church-goer?

2 As well as the accusations of witchcraft, there are other arguments and quarrels among the inhabitants of Salem. Identify as many of these as you can and then construct your impression of their everyday life.

3 There is a clear parallel between the events of 1692 in Salem and the political investigation of the 1950s in America. What are the particular characteristics of this play which make its story timeless and universal?

4 Is John Proctor a hero in his stand against the evil in his society or do you see him as foolish when he might easily have saved his life? Why does he make his individual sacrifice?

5 Arthur Miller says that he was writing about 'an imploded community that distrust and paranoia had killed'. Do you find anything to admire either in the society as a whole or in particular individuals in the play?

Justice and Truth

1 Look again at the second half of Act 4. Elizabeth, Danforth, Hale and Parris all have different views of justice and truth. Can you conclude from these which one the playwright expects us to accept?

2 There is much talk of judging people in this play, as well as a scene in which professional judges conduct their business according to the law. Elizabeth tells John in Act 4 that she cannot judge him and that 'There be no higher judge under Heaven than Proctor is.' What message does all this give us about judging others?

3 The play is set in a theocracy, a religious community, and yet there seems to be controversy about what God expects of people. Look again at what characters such as Danforth, Hale and John and Elizabeth Proctor say about God. How do they agree and how do they differ in their beliefs?

4 The girls are on oath to tell the truth in court. How does their idea of the 'truth' differ from John Proctor's? Does Mary Warren tell the truth or is she merely frightened of Abigail? If you were Abigail could you defend your version of the truth?

5 Is your own view of 'truth' changed by the events in the play?

The importance of one's name

At the beginning of the play Abigail insists to her uncle that 'My name is good in the village! I will not have it said my name is soiled!'

At the end of the play Parris is anxious that John Proctor should sign his confession, saying 'It is a weighty name; it will strike the village that Proctor confess.'

Proctor's own protest is about the value of his own name. 'Because it is my name! Because I cannot have another in my life! Because I lie and sign myself to lies! Because I am not worth the dust on the feet of them that hang! How may I live without my name? I have given you my soul; leave me my name!'

1 Do you think the word 'name' means the same to Abigail, Parris and John Proctor?

2 Why does Proctor refuse to put his name publicly on the document knowing that he will hang as a result?

3 Criticism

1 In *Timebends* Arthur Miller recounts that the strongest objection to his play would be that the Salem witchcraft trials were not a true parallel to the McCarthy investigation. 'There are Communists,' it would repeatedly be said, 'but there were never any witches.' How would you answer this objection?

2 One of the critics (John McClain, *Journal American*), reviewing *The Crucible* after its press-night in January 1953, complained that the story:

'is so far beyond our present concepts of justice and plausible behaviour that I never felt myself part of the proceedings. I never really believed the little monsters that set off the fuse, or that they could make their case stick with the Deputy-Governor of Massachusetts . . . *The Crucible* reveals the same high talent for dialogue, for a well rounded scene as *Death of a Salesman*: I only wish he'd written it around people more understandable.' Do you sympathise with this view or do you find the characters understandable?

3 Two prominent New York theatre critics had diametrically opposing views of the play.

Walter Kerr in the *New York Herald Tribune* thought the play too intellectual. 'It is the intellect which goes out, not the heart . . . You stand back and think; you don't really share very much.'

Richard Watts, Jun. in the *New York Post* wrote:
'Emotionally, I think it is vastly successful. Where I found
it a little disappointing in its final effectiveness is in Mr
Miller's inability to combine with it the kind of intellectual
insight that was so notable in *Death of a Salesman* . . . he
is chiefly concerned with what happened, rather than why,
and this neglect sometimes gives his work a hint of
superficiality.'

Which of these two critical views do you share?

Give plenty of evidence for your opinion.

BIBLIOGRAPHY

Arthur Miller's plays include:

The Man Who Had All the Luck Methuen, 1944
All My Sons Heinemann Educational, 1947
Death of a Salesman Heinemann Educational, 1949
An Enemy of the People (adapted from Ibsen) Nick Hern
   Books, 1950
The Crucible Heinemann Educational, 1953
A Memory of Two Mondays Methuen, 1955
A View From the Bridge Heinemann Educational, 1955
After The Fall Methuen, 1964
Incident at Vichy Methuen, 1964
The Price Methuen, 1968
The Creation of the World and other Business Methuen, 1972
The American Clock Methuen, 1980
The Ride Down Mount Morgan Methuen, 1991

Other works include:

Focus (a novel) Penguin, 1945
The Misfits (a short story, Penguin then a film, then a
   novel) Methuen, 1957 & 1961
Everybody Wins (a screen-play) Methuen, 1990
In Russia (non-fiction) Secker & Warburg, 1969
Chinese Encounters (non-fiction) Farar. Straus. Giroux, 1979
Salesman in Beijing Methuen, 1984
Timebends – A Life (autobiography) Methuen, 1987

Books about Arthur Miller's work include:

Christopher Bigsby (compiler), *File on Miller,* Methuen, 1987
Christopher Bigsby, ed., *Arthur Miller and Company,*
 Methuen, 1990
Neil Carson, *Arthur Miller,* Macmillan, 1982
Robert Corrigan, ed., *Arthur Miller: a collection of critical
 essays,* Prentice Hall, 1969
Bernard F Dukore, *Text and Performance: Death of a Salesman
 and The Crucible,* Macmillan Educational, 1989
John Ferres, ed., *Twentieth-Century interpretations of The
 Crucible,* Prentice Hall, 1972
Dennis Welland, *Miller: A study of his plays,* Oliver & Boyd,
 1961

GLOSSARY

Act One

PAGE

6	*hearty*	well, healthy
7	*heathen*	anyone not Christian; in this case American-Indians
7	*trafficked*	communicated
8	*abominations*	evil things
8	*gibberish*	nonsense
10	*forked and hooved*	the Devil was often portrayed as having an animal's hooves and a forked tail
12	*clamoured intimations*	was disturbed by suspicions
15	*a pointy reckoning*	revenge with a dagger
19	*covenanted*	sworn, contracted Christians
22	*prodigious*	great
24	*Quakers*	members of a religious society (the Society of Friends) founded by George Fox in 1648–50, distinguished by peaceful principles and plainness of dress and manners
25	*break charity*	fall out of friendship
32	*incubi*	evil spirits or demons, usually male
32	*succubi*	evil spirits or demons, usually female

32	*wizards*	men who practise witchcraft
35	*spoke Barbados*	spoke in the language of Barbados and was therefore incomprehensible to the people of Salem
36	*corruptions*	wicked thoughts

Act Two

43	*weighty*	important
43	*the crowd who part like the sea for Israel*	as the sea parted in the Old Testament to allow the Israelites to escape from Egypt
47	*Lucifer*	another name for the devil
48	*commandments*	see the Bible: Deuteronomy 5

1 Thou shalt have no other gods before me.

2 Thou shalt not make unto thee any graven image.

3 Thou shalt not take the name of the Lord in vain.

4 Thou shalt remember the Sabbath Day and keep it holy.

5 Thou shalt honour thy father and thy mother.

6 Thou shalt not kill.

7 Thou shalt not commit adultery.

8 Thou shalt not steal.

9 Thou shalt not bear false witness.

10 Thou shalt not covet thy neighbour's goods.

49	*full to the brim*	well into pregnancy
49	*however single*	even though I am single

52	*it rebels my stomach*	makes me feel ill
53	*Devil's bitch*	an evil spirit
53	*Sabbath day*	Sunday
54	*baptized*	become a part of the church sometimes by immersion in water
57	*the Gospel*	literally, the Good News
59	*misty plot*	blurred, obscured
59	*I'd as lief*	I would rather
60	*signifies*	what does it mean?
61	*a struck beast*	an injured animal
61	*familiar spirit*	an evil spirit
61	*warranted*	needed proof
63	*the keys of the kingdom*	see the Bible: Matthew 16 v19 Christ says to Peter 'And I will give unto thee the keys of the Kingdom of heaven.'
63	*vengeance*	revenge
63	*Pontius Pilate*	John Proctor is here comparing Hale with the Roman official who would find Jesus Christ neither guilty nor innocent of the charges against Him and symbolically washed his hands of the affair
64	*to testify*	to be a witness
65	*blasphemy*	slander, profane speaking
65	*lechery*	committing adultery

Act Three

PAGE

69	*contemptuous*	having no regard for the court
69	*broke charity*	betrayed
69	*affidavit*	a written statement for use in a court
71	*a deposition*	testimony on oath in a court
73	*plough on Sunday*	breaking the fourth commandment
73	*Cain and Abel*	see the Bible: Genesis 4 v8 Cain killed his brother, Abel – the first murder
76	*angel Raphael and Tobias*	this story is in the Apocrypha to the Bible
76	*plaintiff*	one who accuses another in court
79	*effrontery*	insolence
80	*proof so immaculate*	proof without any doubt
80	*ipso facto*	by that very fact (Latin)
81	*probity*	honesty
82	*perjury*	telling lies in court
82	*apparitions*	spectres, phantoms
82	*manifest of the Devil*	a spirit made visible
88	*whore*	prostitute
89	*rung the doom*	announced the ruin, fate
89	*harlot*	prostitute

Act Four

PAGE

97	*Majesty*	in this case, the Devil
100	*contention*	disagreement
100	*providence*	a blessing
101	*faction*	party, conspiracy
103	*beguile*	deceive
104	*adamant*	determined
105	*belie*	to tell lies
106	*cleave*	cling
106	*prevail upon*	persuade
108	*indictment*	charge
109	*gibbet*	gallows, where people were executed by hanging
114	*penitence*	repentance, sorrow for sins